Grand Time

What's the value of life?

Artur Grandi

CONTENTS

WE HANDCRAFT EVERYTHING ON OUR PLANET. *BUT WHAT IS OUR TRUE VALUE?*

Have you ever thought that the world is not fair to us, ordinary people? Have you ever experienced a situation where money or the lack of it took away your dreams? When a smart child, worthy of studying at the most prestigious university, has to get a job to help his parents. When the difference in social status spoils the relationship between two loving hearts. When there is no money to pay for expensive treatment...

Many situations like this can be listed. People face them every day. My loved ones and I have come across such trials repeatedly. Due to this experience I came closer and closer to unraveling the mystery of how to rectify such injustice. As a result, I found a solution to eliminate this chaos without revolutions, without taking from the rich for the benefit of the poor, without inflation. The path I am about to reveal is advantageous for both the affluent and the underprivileged. There is a way to evaluate and reward each person fairly, beyond what they have now.

Soon there will be changes in the financial sphere, and not only there but in all areas of life. In twenty to thirty years, the world will change completely, and new generations won't be able to comprehend what it means to be poor. People will be respected not for the amount of money they have but for who they are and what they bring to the world. Individuals of all backgrounds, regardless of nationality, race, religion, age, or health, will either become wealthy or achieve exceptional prosperity. This signifies that if one aspires to be remarkably affluent, they shall pursue that aspiration, whereas if one prioritizes different values, they will lead a life of affluence and enjoy all they desire.

This book is not only for those who, like me, believe that everyone should be rich and that money should serve people. Even if you don't understand what all this is about quite yet, as you delve into the pages of this book, the meaning will gradually unveil itself: money should serve all of us, regardless of our occupation and the extent of our efforts. Every person on the planet, regardless of their location, appearance, education, or preferences, will have enough money. This will happen, and it is, in fact, already happening.

The unwillingness to have money can be compared to the unwillingness to live. If a person is alive, they have a life. If a person is alive, they have money. People can only lack wealth if they consciously reject it. In future scenarios, there will be no individuals on this planet who find themselves in need of resources to buy food, obtain clean water, secure shelter, or any and all other essentials for a fulfilling life. Allow me to explain how this transformation will occur in simple and understandable language.

We are self-sufficient, and everyone who reads this book attentively will have the opportunity to practically attain wealth. However, there is one crucial aspect. Do not simply accept everything stated. Instead, question what seems unrealistic, reread it, and apply it in practice until you fully comprehend the potential of achieving prosperity and saving the existing financial system from total collapse, elevating it to a new level where money serves people, rather than the other way around. Perhaps, you may have the impression that this method is only for the poor, and that the entire financial world, the world of capitalists and oil magnates, will hinder the enrichment of ordinary people. I dare to dispel these doubts.

Those at the top of the existing financial pyramid are waiting for this remedy even more eagerly. Not literally, of course, as they are more interested in their own, personally accumulated capital. However, these people are more vulnerable to the fear of the current financial pyramid collapsing. They understand very well that if everything remains as it is, a crash is inevitable. Besides, ordinary rich people will spend more and generate more income in all sectors owned by those very magnates.

Let's face the undeniable truth: we are all, in one way or another, slaves. The old slave-owner paradigm has evolved, but it still exists today. Even the wealthiest individuals on the planet are enslaved by the pursuit of money. The middle class enjoys a degree of freedom, but we, the financially deprived (those of us who struggle from paycheck to paycheck or have next to nothing), bear the least burden of financial servitude. If you don't agree with this assertion, I will provide the evidence in one of the upcoming chapters. The absence of money is, first of all, a manifestation of disagreement with the injustice of our existing system. Deep inside, we all realize that it shouldn't be this way. As you read through the entirety of the book, everything will become clear.

1

THE DIVE

This book delves into a formula designed to cure our ailing financial system. This formula, though seemingly uncomplicated, demands contemplation and time for its full comprehension. Those who are in a hurry can find the formula in the book's conclusion. However, I affirm that true understanding and, more importantly, practical implementation necessitate revisiting the beginning and immersing yourself in each chapter.

Each word written in this book is born of lived experience. Every fact, every name, every corporate entity is drawn from the real world, and I bear the full weight of responsibility for every statement. In simpler terms, I stand by each word. The lessons derived from the turbulent nineties were not in vain; this book offers real-world, actionable insights.

But let's proceed methodically. I want to make it clear that I don't possess any academic degrees in the realm of finance. Everything I've accomplished has been through my personal journey of trial and error, spanning my entire conscious life. If you take a glance at my social media profile and spot the owner of the Riviera football club in Sochi, don't be surprised—that's me. If you happen to recognize the carpenter in the picture installing a window in your house, and I hope that window is still standing there—yes, that's me as well. I would like to apologize for my linguistic shortcomings to anyone who might identify me as the plumbing expert in Chicago. I can also be recognized as the owner of Grand Comfort, a Chicago-based company that has experienced a remarkable transformation with an annual revenue surge from a modest hundred thousand to an impressive two million dollars within a mere two years under my guidance.

The list doesn't end here. You may recognize me as the CEO of SochiGrandStroi development corporation; a taxi driver—I hope you liked the journey with the dulcet sound of Mozart; the proprietor of the free weekly newspaper Sochi Boulevard with a hundred thousand copies in circulation; the co-founder of the Grand Time fund in the state of Delaware, focused on financing innovative startups that are reshaping the deferred profit market.

These are just a few of my transformations, each accompanied by painful emotions, dissent, and the relentless quest for the elixir to cure the rapidly deteriorating financial system. The numerous falls and rises endowed me with a wealth of practical knowledge and I can share a panoramic view of the chaos that ensnares the world of finance. What is even more important—I am the person who can provide the compass to navigate towards the remedy required for the recovery of the whole financial system.

To create a bond of trust, I open the door to my innermost chambers, revealing secrets which are unknown even to my close companions. I invoke the reader to be frank and fair when I ask questions in an intimate conversation. I address you personally, as if conversing with myself. I assure you that the book remains impervious to your personal information. It acts as a mirror reflecting your own truths. Reading these pages constitutes a dialogue with your very essence.

I wish to bring to your attention a mention of an existing bonus in the book designed as a living testament to the formula's efficacy. Consider the Grand bonus as one of the practical applications of this formula. I hope that following the formula's introduction, alternative bonuses from other projects will emerge, and I perceive them not as rivals but as companions, supported by our Grand Time foundation. As long as they uphold the core principles of the formula designed to cure our ailing financial system.

In this chapter we are speaking about the dive. Why do we need it? Let me begin with an example. During my school years, I was not able to run long distances. Regardless of the position, simply crossing the finish line was a monumental achievement. My PE teacher, Andrey Ardovazdovich, used to say, "Try running at a more leisurely pace, and success will inevitably follow." In my case, it wasn't a lack of breath that hindered me but a profound misunderstanding of an elementary concept. Two decades later, when I laced up my running shoes, I completed an eleven-kilometer run without gasping for breath. It gave me a thrill. Merely by adopting a slower stride, as my teacher had told me, I could have become the frontrunner at school. Ah, if only I had deciphered the teacher 's words earlier...

Thanks to this childhood experience and later interactions with investors in Silicon Valley, I realized that sometimes it can be difficult to explain even the simplest concepts. It's not about the brains; it's about the willingness to understand. The fact is, I didn't have that desire. I never wanted to become a runner. The most important thing is to be ready to accept the necessary information. The information contained in this book is essential for the majority of the world's population. Anyone who absorbs it can become wealthy and contribute to the healing of the existing financial system.

People are eager to grasp these ideas, yet they are held back by a fear of change. I guarantee changes for everyone who uses the information practically. To do so, you'll need to dedicate at least fifteen minutes to yourself each day and engage in your favorite activity. It sounds simple, right? Don't jump to conclusions too quickly. My experience with running has taught me that speed doesn't always guarantee reaching the finish line.

Now, let's take a closer look at the current reality. We live on a planet where everything necessary for a luxurious life for many generations ahead is available. Technology allows us to fully provide the population of the planet with all it needs: housing, food, and equipment. There is more than enough money to ensure this provision. So, why do the majority of people on Earth live in poverty? The answer is simple: the financial system is not ready for change; it is entirely outdated and needs an upgrade. To usher in an era of abundance, we need to finance the "construction" of all mentioned benefits. The only thing is, we're not entirely prepared to accept these gifts. Who will provide them for us?

Truthfully, there is no hidden secret here. The foundation of this formula is grounded in the collective experience of countless generations: the act of giving leads to abundance. This concept has its roots in history, dating back to the birth of the American dollar. America extended loans to nations in need at minimal interest rates and, in return, its currency gained popularity. This popularity led to a surge in its value and the esteemed status of a global superpower.

It is crucial to remember, however, that blindly giving and recklessly printing more money can be disastrous, as it can incite unhealthy competition between nations, often resulting in wars and bringing suffering to innocent people. It is yet another testament to the fact that the prevailing global financial system has outlived its utility. In our case, the givers are ordinary individuals who grasp the essence of this formula. So, you might ask, "Where will these individuals find the resources needed for such generosity?"

As I've mentioned earlier, everyone should have access to money, but I haven't explained how it's achievable yet. I would say that it is not only simple but also pleasurable since it involves individuals engaging in activities they love while acquiring Grand bonuses. (That's what we call our formula for revitalizing the existing financial system.) Remember the "fifteen minutes a day" I mentioned earlier? That was just a benchmark, the rest is up to you.

Everything stated here has been thoroughly tested in practice. For instance, if you enjoy learning a language, you can join a special study group. There's no need to pay for the education—you'll receive bonuses for your actions because teachers are also pursuing their passion and earning bonuses. If psychology is your interest, there are groups dedicated to that as well—you can collect your bonuses there. If you love spending time on social media, it's possible to acquire bonuses in that sphere as well. I know it's hard to believe at this point, but it's a fact.

Those in the financial world can grasp the concepts I'm describing here with ease. However, the fear of change not only clouds their common sense but also distorts their logic regarding the topics under discussion. Fear is a powerful force for controlling people. Everyone uses it, even as they fall into the trap of the existing financial system themselves. To be more precise, they fall into the trap of their own deception. However, let's discuss fear later. First, we need to tackle the elimination of deception.

2

ERADICATING DECEPTION

Deception is everywhere, so deeply ingrained in our lives that we often fail to recognize it. We live in a world of lies and, most importantly, we lie to ourselves, believing that we are happy.

What exactly do we mean when we use the word "happiness?" It is a particular state that accompanies us through a multitude of situations, coupled with intense emotions, euphoria, a dance of butterflies, a harmonious melody of joy, satisfaction, self-esteem, and a desire to share happiness with everyone around.

When do we experience these emotions? These occurrences can happen at various moments, spanning from the simple relief of releasing one's bladder after a long wait to the gratification experienced after making a long-cherished dream purchase. There's no guarantee that one will bring more joy than the other.

As an example, let me tell you about an incident that left an indelible mark on my life. The joyful eyes and emotions of a person I saw in the pre-holiday city hustle literally turned my perception of happiness upside down. He had no fixed residence—his tattered clothing, unpleasant odor, and painful thinness spoke of it. Homelessness doesn't exist in all countries, but if it does, it's often ignored. This serves as confirmation of a universal deception. We frequently pay more attention and care to animals and plants in our gardens than to people perishing before our eyes. I not only take notice but also engage in conversations with such individuals. Most of them have broad worldviews, personal convictions, and their own philosophies. First and foremost, they are people and only then are they homeless. In the harsh reality of early 2000s Russia, where happy faces were considered a sign of foolishness or detachment, that man couldn't hide his smile. He radiated pure happiness, even though he had no roof over his head, was hungry, and couldn't predict when he would eat next. But he was certain—that night he would sleep on a soft mattress. He had found it in a dump and carried it to his makeshift dwelling. Why did this incident leave an unforgettable impression on me? I caught myself thinking that, at that moment, I wasn't a happy person, despite being a completely fulfilled family man, a successful entrepreneur, an industry leader with nothing to complain about. But my subconscious kept telling me, "You can do more." What could I do? At that time, it was impossible to understand; I still had a long journey ahead.

Allow me to illustrate it with one more example from the city of Sochi. The military had been unable to construct a particular building for fifteen years due to a minor permit-related issue. I was aware of this project and decided to undertake its construction. The city authorities trusted me and granted permission during the documentation process. Within ten months, we created a ten-story building on Tonnelnaya Street. People finally got their long-awaited apartments, the military reported back to their superiors, workers earned their wages, and the company gained its profit. Yet, I couldn't grasp the sensation of happiness.

Though I had likely experienced it countless times during the construction process, finding happiness in each moment, the specific kind of joy associated with a significant culmination or momentous achievement evaded me. I even felt somewhat melancholic about parting with this long-awaited event. Ultimately, it was just another project, completed and set into motion.

So, what are we chasing? Money, fame, power. Yet, it sounds as if we are pursuing happiness, chasing our dreams. That's another deception...

People often fail to distinguish between dreams and the relentless pursuit of material gain. Based on my personal observations, the majority of individuals choose their professions with one primary focus: wealth, fame, and power. For example, when I picture myself as a doctor, I see the patient's eyes, his life hanging in the balance, and I eagerly rush to aid him. All this is about power, and we'll explore the concept of it in a different chapter.

I've heard such statements even from renowned doctors. In interviews, they speak about their practice and highlight such examples. In other words, they relish the moment when someone's life rests in their hands. Surprisingly, the formula designed to cure the existing financial system unveils reality in its purest and most honest form. It will help us to discover our true essence when there's no longer a need to deceive ourselves and those around us.

If we take responsibility and understand that we are part of this universal lie, then we have a better chance to change the world.

From an early age, we give instructions to our children. They must attend school, do their homework, and be obedient. We also instill in them the belief that they owe a debt to their homeland, an obligation that may even demand fighting and sacrificing their lives for their country—an absurdity we teach our children ourselves. This leads to the crucial question: to whom do our children truly owe this obligation?

We shatter their individual thinking from a young age with our own falsehoods. We rejoice when we manage to convince a child that Santa Claus is real. I admit that I also fell into this trap, succumbing to Kristina's [my wife] persuasion, and I regret it to this day. I hope the realization of the fact that Santa Claus is just an ordinary person in a costume hasn't led my children to the belief that they can't trust me.

Raf and Olya have the freedom to ask me any question, and they will always receive an honest answer. When Raf was in the sixth grade, he came to me with a question related to the topic of drugs they had recently covered at school. Having noticed my profound knowledge, he asked me a direct question, "Dad, were you a drug addict?" That was a challenging moment, and I struggled to respond. He recalls it with a smile, recounting how his father suddenly turned into a child desperately trying to justify himself.

However, I found the strength within me to provide an honest answer. I told him, "Yes, I was a complete drug addict." But the conversation didn't stop there. He delved into the details, asking me what I used and how I managed to become a functioning member of society after such a past. He also learned that many friends of mine had tragically passed away. Being as honest as possible with my loved ones has always been crucial to me.

In fact, this honesty played a vital role in my journey from a troubled past to becoming a respected individual whom my children are proud of. As I carved my path to success, it was essential for my clients to trust me. The projects I undertook were worth hundreds of millions, and all my clients were aware of my tarnished past. I simply remained honest with them, and they placed their trust in me.

How will the formula help to eliminate lies? It's as simple as can be. By obtaining bonuses for actions, we help the world to heal itself in both financial and non-financial aspects. Each of us will feel our unique value, and the fear of losing a job will disappear. This chain reaction will ripple through all spheres of life, making truth-telling the new norm. We will transition into a state of equilibrium and bask in a world tailored for our genuine selves. We will return to a normal state and will live in the world which is made for us.

Let's be honest with ourselves. Let's stop ignoring the poor or telling our children that a homeless person has a choice and he himself decides to be in that situation. With the healing of the system, the option of having a choice will indeed become available to anyone willing to change their life.

Again, I urge you to contemplate what we are discussing! It has become our norm to be immersed in deception in every aspect of life. Let me give you an example. Each employee of a grocery store understands to some extent that the goods on the shelves are often poisoned. How, you may ask, does this happen? The farmer, striving for profit, adds chemicals to the potatoes for increased yield, and everyone on the farm knows it, being part of the deception. Potatoes are transported to the chip factory, and again everyone is involved in the communal lies: at the loading docks, on the scales, with the gasoline for transportation—at every possible juncture. How many professions participating in this deception have we touched upon?

Let's continue. The chip factory transforms one kilo of potatoes into five kilos of chips. Potatoes are bland and tasteless when cooked at home, but when turned into chips, they exude the aroma of rustic homegrown crops. That's because chemists and biologists join the deception. They add flavor enhancers that induce addiction, while marketers create colorful packaging made from toxic materials that pollute the planet... Shall I go on?

I believe that you've seized the essence: this pattern can be applied to any domain.

Take those high-end stores offering eco-friendly products. Their purity might be up for debate, but the real issue lies elsewhere. People lacking sufficient funds are forced to settle for substandard food. All of us are funding this chaos.

Everyone should have access to clean and healthy products. Food should be abundant just like all other essentials for every human being on this planet. It's a completely achievable goal, and it will be accomplished as part of the revitalization of the existing financial system. The old system has neglected to recognize the value of its human resources. It's important to point out that without us, there would be no chips, farms, factories, or stores. No one would be there to finance them or work for them, which means they wouldn't exist.

The fundamental rule of the bonus system is "giving leads to prosperity." This means the valued human resource is gradually infused into the old system in small portions, entering into a relationship with the old system and, therefore, updating it.

3

THE COST OF LIFE

I understand that the title of this chapter may provoke many questions and much criticism. However, there's only one reason for such a response. The dying financial system is not competent in this matter: it loudly proclaims that human life is priceless and cannot be quantified in monetary terms. It's true—in the current system, a person's life is not measured by a certain amount of money, however, their labor is. In other words, "live as you wish, we'll only pay for your labor." This perspective is fundamentally flawed. It's commonly believed that the basis of the economy is money, and we pay money for everything. Only not our own—we're given money temporarily and we are obliged to return it later.

Life is priceless, but with money you can release a criminal from prison, while without it, they remain incarcerated. I apologize for my emotions. I recognize that I frequently repeat these simple truths. In life, I've explained them countless times, only to hear people say, "I just don't understand you." Nobody's to blame for that. This is the consequence of the belief that human life is beyond any price.

People evaluate everything: animals, natural resources, water, plots of land, but they've forgotten about themselves. To change this sad situation, the formula for healing the existing financial system was created. It can honestly and clearly calculate the cost of the entire human resource and the cost of each individual. After this evaluation, a miracle happens: by engaging in any activity, we obtain our own bonuses. They belong only to us because they are generated through our actions. No one gives them or takes them away; we distribute them by buying goods and services thus growing rich.

This reminds me of a tradition in my family which probably dates back to ancient times. My grandmother and later my mother put a bracelet on the wrist of every newborn in our family from the moment of their birth. My grandmother used to say it was to protect the babies from the evil eye, to keep them from getting sick. After forty days, the bracelet could be removed, and the baby was placed under the protection of higher powers. She claimed that sometimes the little stones on the bracelet needed to be replaced. They occasionally broke due to someone's envious eyes, effectively absorbing all the negative energy. She even knew which stone had been on my father's bracelet since his birth, placed by my great-grandmother.

I believe that soon all children will have bracelets that allow them to earn bonuses just for being themselves. These bonuses will be awarded for their very existence, their breath, their life, and their growth. While this may represent a minimal income, it's a step in the right direction. The formula will calculate far fewer bonuses for a minute of a baby's life than for a minute of hard work, but you can imagine how valuable these bonuses will be when people start using them.

This technology already exists, and many people use smartwatches with pulse measurement, breath monitoring, and motion tracking. The function can easily be connected to the bonus wallet, allowing people to start earning bonuses from the moment they're born. For the readers of the new generation, there won't even be questions about the pricelessness of life. In the new system, human life is evaluated in terms of honest currency, Grand bonuses, and people are the foundation of the global economy. So, my friends, it's time to cherish yourselves. I've already taken the first step in doing this.

How I came to the idea that money should serve people

In moments of despair many people give up due to their own helplessness. Everything seems to be against them. Swift changes often alter their social circle and distance them from once-close friends and family. However, there are those who, instead of giving into despair, radically change their lives and become successful entrepreneurs, scientists, and athletes.

I don't belong to any of these categories. I've always had a desire to help people, especially those close to me. I've always wanted to inspire people, to help them achieve the results they craved together. I believe that we can't be truly happy when we reach great heights but lose the connection with our loved ones in the meantime.

I only blame myself in all my misfortunes, learn my lessons and keep going forward. As a side note, in any situation, including moments of despair, my favorite phrase is "let's move forward." I'm sure you've already guessed that the formula for the new financial system came to me through tough times, financial crashes, and life lessons that I've experienced.

The accumulated life experience has cost me a lot. Its value is measured in time. When I provide consultations to those who seek them, people elevate to new income levels or discover new skills within themselves. It's immeasurable, but the gratitude I receive always surpasses the fee.

Where was God?

I didn't even know God when I I had an argument with Him for the first time. I stood in front of the icons and yelled at the top of my lungs accusing Him of injustice. I remember that moment vividly: I shouted that things shouldn't be this way, questioning what kind of God He was if He couldn't make people happy. I accompanied this outburst with some colorful profanities.

I'm not encouraging anyone to repeat my experience, but I'll say, from that very moment until today, we understand each other. Even though He guides me through life silently and without explanations. After every fall, I always ask Him the same question, "What do I need that for?"

I realized one truth—everything that happens in our life is for our benefit. All situations are given to protect us from mistakes and to move each person toward their destiny.

This reminds me of a parable; I can't reproduce it word for word, but I'll convey the essence. After death, a person met God and asked Him, "Why didn't you help me when I was in trouble?" In response, God showed the person's life path—human footprints could be seen along with the traces of God there. The person examined it closely and pointed, "At this very moment I was suffering greatly, but I don't see Your footprints here." The answer came immediately, "There are no footprints of yours because at that very moment I was carrying you."

The same thing happens in our lives. The Universe always helps each of us in our life's journey. I appeal to skeptics and atheists who'll probably ask, "Then why do children die prematurely?" We, people, live in a material world and want all the answers to be confirmed by facts. That being said, we only inhabit our bodies for a tiny fraction of our existence.

We only come into the material world for a few seconds. That would stay true even if we were able to live on Earth for two hundred years. The mission of the child, who passed on prematurely, could have been to help his loved ones endure their lesson, subsequently enabling them to fulfill their life's purpose. Any person who sees death as a journey is capable of bringing knowledge into our material world and making it better.

During a moment of despair and disagreement with God, I came to the idea that money should serve people and be accessible to everyone. Through my own experience, I vividly realized that working for twelve hours a day made me a hostage to the existing system and I had to change it. Now, after twenty-five years, I don't consider the word "change" appropriate—I believe that it's more about healing, improving, and making changes that suit the current time and the modern people.

At the age of twenty-four, I already had a family of my own, including a one-year-old son. I faced harsh reality—it was difficult to provide my loved ones even with the most basic necessities. I remember the shame I felt in front of my wife when I realized that she had secretly been giving me money borrowed from her relatives because she didn't want to hurt my pride. My parents also helped us with everything they could: shelter, food, and covering utility bills. Despite all this support, my factory worker's salary was insufficient.

That's when I realized the most important thing: we are all slaves to money. It shouldn't be that way! I made a firm decision to change this system and take control of money. Back then, I lacked the vast experience I can share now, twenty-five years later, but my unwavering determination, self-confidence, and ambition allowed me, a worker in a small municipal division, to start my own company.

Established by me in 1998, SochiGrandStroi managed the entire housing and utilities complex in the city of Sochi and undertook construction projects across Southern Russia. The company had an annual turnover of one and a half billion rubles, and it employed over two thousand five hundred people. Unfortunately, I was not happy. I was proud of my accomplishments, but the idea of changing the financial system that enslaved people seemed unreal at that time. In those years, I promoted and advised everyone around me for free. I invested my time and gained immense satisfaction from the results.

What makes me keep conveying the information that, as I thought, everyone knew but no one paid attention to or valued? It's the satisfaction of my own ego which will soar to the heavens and rejoice every day until the end of my life once I'm heard. What else should a person feel if thousands of people are truly happy?

During the period of my company's success, many people, who were simple workers or plumbers at the time, became deputies, officials, prosperous entrepreneurs, businessmen, and overall wealthy individuals due to my guidance and support. I even achieved the impossible: the rates for repairs and maintenance of housing in the city of Sochi remained unchanged for five years. I engaged in charity and raised salaries. But all of this seemed to be a drop in the ocean, compared to my ambitious goal. I wasn't alone on this path; I found like-minded individuals, and the number of these people grows every day.

Then the depression came, but I recall it with gratitude. I lost everything, or better say, my business—as there was nothing else. I didn't even have the time to buy a couple of apartments to later rent out, which I could have easily afforded before my business was gone. My wife still reminds me of that since she was the one that came up with that idea. I assured her not to worry, as I had managed to acquire a sand and gravel quarry that would support our family until retirement. Unfortunately, later on we lost the quarry as well.

However, during this challenging period, I acquired much more, vastly more, some might even say, incomparably more than ever. The idea of the new financial system emerged from my disagreement with the existing one. The knowledge, which I gladly share in this book, came from my experience, tears, and mistakes. It's not even knowledge —it's a practical guide that can be used to achieve results.

What's the idea?

Money is essential for our transactions, merely serving as a tool in our hands. The crucial part: we have it.

But let's start from the beginning. For decades, we've witnessed currency inflation in practically all countries. This primarily speaks of imperfect market mechanisms. It reflects the citizens' mistrust of governmental figures ensuring currency stability and skepticism towards banks, financial institutions, exchanges, and other components of the financial world.

This mistrust usually appears on a subconscious level. After all, the majority of people don't think about it, but when they come to the store for groceries, they pay a higher price each year. At the same time, earning a living becomes more and more challenging in many countries. All of us are observers and even participants in the slow and steady destruction of the global financial system.

How can we stop the decline, stabilize it, and enable growth? How can we simultaneously support the entire financial system and significantly increase the income of ordinary people? Some readers might think that it's too global. Yes, that's right, but we've already started the process. Could one really think that a formula for healing the financial system appeared without experience and evidence? Of course it couldn't be applied in practice without proof. We have already done so—every participant of the experiment sees the result in their own wallet.

Allow me to share a so-called review from one of the participants of our project: "I joined completely by chance. Over time all my friends and acquaintances started asking me how I managed to look younger, where I got all this energy, humor, zest for life, which cosmetologists I was visiting and how much money I inherited."

At that time, the bonuses were just figures on our website. Still, after the question of what actually happened, the participant replied, "I allowed myself to dream" and added that for many years, she hadn't allowed herself to do that. "I thought my whole life would pass in the hustle between work, household chores, and other everyday concerns. When I started dedicating fifteen minutes a day to myself, miraculously, more time appeared in my hands and, eventually, I allowed myself to dream. That's when my life started to change; people around me began to notice my mood. They reached out to me with job offers, invitations to events, and friendship. I noticed that I stopped being average and became a bright and sought-after personality."

This is a fact. We change and the world around us changes too. When we earn money for our well-being through the right actions— step by step—we heal the entire global financial system.

A wealthy acquaintance of mine used to say, "You can't earn all the money in the world." Perhaps he was unaware of a simple thing: if all the money resides in one place, it loses its value. Money that is not in circulation ceases to be in demand because there is no supply. The value of such money is zero. It's like a scenario where the government prints money but forgets to put it into circulation, and a pile of paper banknotes just takes up space in storage. Allow me to remind you that two percent of the world's population owns fifty percent of all the money.

My book, by no means, advocates taking from the rich and giving to the poor. It doesn't call for the wealthy to inject more money into circulation. Unfortunately, they can't do that because they are hostages of the financial system. If they loosen their purse strings, inflation will develop at a faster pace, ultimately leading the world to recession and the destruction of the financial system even more rapidly. Now we understand: the richer a person is, the harder it is to adapt to the new format of an honest financial system, no matter how much they desire it.

The new system is designed to gradually update or heal the old one which is halfway destroyed, without abrupt and large-scale actions. Everyone will benefit from this transition. As I mentioned before, first we need to understand that money created for transactions should be accessible to everyone. To achieve this, it's important to evaluate each of our actions correctly. From birth to death we perform various actions without receiving any bonuses, except for our wages. I can imagine the questions that will come up here. You may ask who will pay for these "actions." And even if we find such a fool, how will these actions be assessed? And if they are assessed, how will they be calculated? Even if all of the above is possible, how will our daily actions generate income? Take it easy. Let's go step by step.

One of my potential investors lectured me on this in the past. "A person should earn money for the work done only if the results of his work can be sold at a higher price. If a worker in a bakery makes one hundred pies, he will receive a salary and the owner of the bakery will sell the pies and make a profit." Correct, but that's only true according to the rules of the current financial system that is dying. My head was occupied with other thoughts, and I saw no point in trying to convince him. I was thinking about how to show the obvious to people—that way there would be no need to persuade anyone. This was the task I approached for twenty-five years and discovered the correct formula given in this book.

We always need to remember: we are the most valuable resource. All pies, roads, theaters are created by human hands and at our expense. The cost of pies should also only be determined after taking that into consideration. Now it is clear that the evaluation of the human resource from birth to death is the missing factor that falls to the base of the formula for healing the existing financial system.

4

MONEY AND BANKS

The history of the origin of money is entirely understandable and in our time seems logical. Since ancient civilizations people have used money for the exchange of goods and services. A fisherman would catch fish and exchange part of the catch for wheat, so that bread would appear on his table. This was extremely challenging because each of them had their own perception of the value of fish and wheat. A farmer from a neighboring village could exchange a bucket of wheat for the fish, or instead for just a bowl. When money emerged as a unit of measurement, it became easier and more convenient to exchange goods. It didn't matter whether the money was made of wood, iron, copper, or gold. What mattered was its purpose: to facilitate the exchange of goods and services. The seller has the goods, the buyer has the money—they exchange and go their own ways.

Today there is a lack of one important factor—transparency. Complete transparency of the transaction ensures full trust. Price tags displayed openly used to contribute to trust. You could compare prices and the quality of goods from different sellers. This simple and straightforward system should remain unchanged, understandable, and transparent for all people to this day.

When we go to the bank to open an account, we are asked for identification documents and if we don't provide them, the account won't be opened. This is a normal and natural condition for a bank—to know our details. But do we know what this bank has in its safe?

Transparency and openness should be equal on both sides of any transaction. Banking experts may object and present quite understandable arguments. There are banking reports that can be studied if one desires to understand what assets a particular bank possesses. Yes, this cannot be denied; there are reports, as well as regulations that allow banks to dispose of our money, lending it out at interest. And it's no secret to anyone that any, even the largest bank in the world, will collapse overnight if depositors decide to withdraw their savings. We often witness such cases nowadays. How does it happen? According to regulations, the bank distributes money to its clients. Even if all is legally sound and these clients have passed all verification steps, the bank essentially has no sums issued as loans. This also complies with norms and rules until the moment the sum of depositors' claims exceeds the limits, and the bank is forced to admit its insolvency.

In my practice, I had a sad experience when I left people without their salaries. I consider that yet another situation that both caused me suffering and provided me with a clue for defining the formula to heal the existing financial system. The evening before payday, especially during the holiday season, everyone usually has an uplifted mood and grand plans. People get ready for the celebration, buy gifts, and, as usual, this leads to extra expenses. The scale of my enterprise allowed me to choose which bank to open an account with, and the local bank managers in the city of Sochi competed for such significant privileges. However, the salaries of the employees of such a large enterprise amounted to a substantial sum. On the day that one of my major clients did not settle the bill on time, I went to the bank for a loan and it turned out that, for formal reasons, the bank wouldn't be able to help us with said loan.

This perfectly describes one-sidedly advantageous acquaintances: we are open to banks and they even manage our money, but we are only allowed to accept or reject their terms. As it soon became clear, this bank was on the verge of bankruptcy. At that time I had to sell my only personal asset—a sand and gravel quarry—and deposit all the money earned into the cash register to pay people their salaries. But even this turned out to be insufficient, and I had to mortgage my parents' house. By the way, during the bankruptcy procedure of that very MezhPromBank, my own house was arrested by the court and put up for auction without even covering the entire debt amount. That's how blind trust in the existing financial system can turn out. But, as I've mentioned before, I was fortunate to have such vivid life lessons to progress toward the main goal.

Many years later, while in America, I spent a year in the Silicon Valley which is commonly considered the center of the financial system. During numerous meetings with representatives of funds, I formulated the missing elements for the formula designed to heal the existing system.

The good news lies in the transparency of the formula. Everything is simple, as in the most ancient times. Any inhabitant on the planet can look into the repository, that is, into the public database, and see all the bonuses that have existed in the world since the first bonus was mined in history. You can see how many bonuses are in the accounts of their owners only without their names. It's possible to observe the amount of bonuses obtained per hour, per day, per week. You can know how many of them will be mined in a day, in a year, and even in a century. Anyone interested in that can enter the repository and see it with their own eyes. The complete transparency of the system provides full trust.

Another piece of good news lies in the fact that the bonus wallet for any user has a deposit storage function. That is, you can choose a storage period—for example, one year—and the system will show how many bonuses can be obtained as gratitude after this period. Please, don't rush to criticize. The main point is that all bonuses, along with gratitude, remain on our balances for this entire year, just like a frozen asset. The system is absolutely transparent and understandable for such operations, among others. Our money is not lent to other people; it is stored in our accounts along with the dividends prepared in advance for payment. This is beneficial for everyone and increases the liquidity of the bonus.

Many bankers have already realized that banks won't survive without transparency. They are introducing convenient applications, reducing overstaffed departments, and these are only the first steps towards system recovery. In the end, we will trust banks thanks to their transparency and openness. We will use money that survives after getting rid of lies through the implementation of the bonus system. In the long run, truth can bring more than falsehood—that is the most important thing.

5

THE COST OF BONUS

"How much will I be paid?" That is a question that people constantly ask. Some more often, some less. There are situations when I forget that I need to earn money. It's a rare occurrence—to see a specialist who is passionate enough about an idea to forget to discuss the cost of work. I usually pay more than the declared cost to such professionals because they are masters of their craft. Money is the bonus they receive for their favorite pastime.

Please note, I'm not talking about the bonus created to heal the existing financial system, but it does operate in the same manner. We obtain it beyond ordinary rewards—in addition to salaries, in our free time doing what we love, raising children or working at home. Each person seeks and chooses their own direction. By earning bonuses, we contribute to healing the existing system—creating a foundation in the form of an assessed human resource. Who will evaluate it? How is the cost of the bonus formed?

Market mechanisms have survived in the modern world since the time when price tags appeared. The cost in the market is regulated based on demand and supply. When coming to the market for tomatoes, our ancestors could see the offers of all sellers on the shelves, compare the prices and quality of tomatoes, persuade the seller to give a discount, and buy the best product at the lowest cost. This simple, transparent system does not need changes and lives to this day. We ourselves determine the cost in the market: we buy tomatoes or wait for the right price.

Grand Bonus, like any currency, commodity, or service, is evaluated by the market. That is, by us. There are many currencies in the markets, and their value depends on demand. So, we evaluate all these currencies. Brokers, traders, bankers—they are also among us. Why do you think almost all currencies are subject to inflation? That's because we stop valuing them, understanding their true worth, though sometimes subconsciously. Will the value of a bonus, backed by your own actions and belonging to you, represent worth for you? I hope that the answer is obvious: you will certainly appreciate it.

I'm going to tell you a story from my childhood that is particularly fitting for this chapter. I was eight years old when my parents sent me to my grandmother Aza for summer vacation. Her full name was Nvard, but everyone called her Aza. I begged her to go to the village to visit her sister, since I loved spending time with Dima, who, although he was my uncle, was only two years older than me. Yerchan, his mom, was just about to go to the market to sell cheese she made from their own cow's milk. I was lucky, and I went with Dima to help her. She was superstitious and warned us that if she didn't sell all the cheese by the evening, she wouldn't take us to the market with her anymore. Imagine her surprise when, even before we could set up the cheese on the counter, she sold it for a higher price than she had planned. A miracle? No. It's a normal situation in market relations: there was high demand for cheese that day, and there were few cheese sellers. When we came, they bought all our cheese in bulk. We made more money than we had planned because buyers were willing to pay a higher price for the cheese.

The value of the Grand Bonus can be depicted for amusement, allowing the reader, upon opening the book in ten years, to calculate the percentage of its growth. Or shed a tear for the missed opportunities if they started mining the bonus much later. I intentionally avoid comparing the value of the bonus to other currencies; any reader will understand its approximate value by comparing the prices of goods and services exchanged by participants of the experiment. For example, at the moment, in different directions, we mine up to ten thousand Grand bonuses per week, spending about twenty hours doing what we love in our free time. With ten thousand bonuses you can buy a women's handbag, wall clocks, wash a car or take an English language course.

People who trade these currencies show interest in comparing the value of the bonus with other currencies. These are the individuals who have been tracking the value of the Grand Bonus on exchanges, studying price charts, activity, and other liquidity indicators to place bets and trade. In this chapter it is important to understand how the value is formed. It is formed precisely by that ancient tool—a market mechanism, due to the demand of buyers and the supply of sellers. In other words, the buyer must choose our bonuses out of all the "tomatoes" offered in the market. It would be more correct to say that buyers should have bonuses in their wallets, and sellers should have the desire and ability to receive them for their goods.

A significant role in the value of goods and services is played by advertising; I believe a separate chapter should be dedicated to this sphere. For example, a story about which meadows a cow grazes on and how it receives a massage before milking to prevent udder pain can influence the cost of milk or cheese. This is product advertising, which has gained considerable influence in all kinds of today's markets, from selling tomatoes to presidential elections.

The good news is that the bonus system is in the early stages of its development. This means that with each subsequent stage, the bonus will gain more popularity by adding programs in various fields of activity for bonus mining. Adding goods and services to the bonus wallet store will also impact the development of the bonus system's popularity and, consequently, influence the value of the bonus itself through tools such as:

1. Deposit storage system.
2. Earning bonuses for attracting active users.
3. Time-limited bonus distribution.
4. Exchanging bonuses for goods and services.
5. Investing bonuses in a profitable business supported by the bonus wallet algorithms.

I anticipate a question from a specific category of people who usually say, "I still don't understand how much the bonus is worth." These people actually realize everything but are subject to the fear of change, and they are in mild shock and confusion that everything is so simple, and that the time for change has already come. However, people are not ready to quit their backbreaking jobs and dive headfirst into something new because starting from scratch is daunting. I have two pieces of good news for such people. The first is—they don't have to quit anything. The second—they can gradually start mastering their favorite activity in their free time and leave their backbreaking job only after being confident in the stability of the new income.

But let me get to the point.

The true value of the Grand bonus is assessed by one criterion —the average amount mined per minute. You can observe the mining cost scale in the bonus wallet. This scale displays the average time it takes to obtain one Grand bonus because mining is time-limited and obtaining more than ten million in a day is impossible. Thus, if ten million people were mining bonuses daily, on average, each person could mine one bonus. You can check another indicator at any moment and track how many bonuses were mined in the past minute by all users.

Another indicator helps determine how many users were simultaneously mining bonuses during that specific minute. In digital terms, with an overall average mining rate of seven thousand bonuses per minute by all seven thousand users simultaneously, the mining cost for one user is one bonus per minute. Of course, this is an average market value as there are twenty difficulty levels, meaning that a baby could mine significantly fewer bonuses in a minute than someone engaged in physical labor.

These completely understandable indicators provide the opportunity for a correct assessment of the market value without the influence of advertising mechanisms. A thoughtful investor, upon seeing these indicators, can determine when it is advantageous to purchase a bonus. It's important to understand another fact: it's advantageous for us to start mining bonuses at any moment because with each subsequent day, the mining cost will depend on the number of miners, and as it's known, our numbers increase every day. This is good news in every sense because along with the difficulties of mining, demand will increase. If it's possible to mine one bonus per minute now, and in a month it's possible to mine 0.1 bonuses per minute, that won't mean that in a month you won't be able to buy the same item for 0.1 bonuses as you can buy today for one. For example, with ten million miners per minute one person will be able to mine approximately 0.00069 bonuses.

As it is known, demand raises the value.

6

BACKING THE BONUS WITH TIME

I believe the reader has been eagerly awaiting for the formula mentioned in this book. But please, be patient. Everything comes in its own time.

Time is the resource we possess from birth to death; nobody can take it away. It's the guarantee behind the bonus obtained by an individual.

For more than five years I have been hosting live broadcasts in the Grand Time community. People often asked me when I would write a book, and I did, in fact, have such an intention. I even outlined the approximate content. Yet, for some reason I couldn't start writing, as if something very important was missing. Then one day everything clicked all at once! I felt a rush of emotions that simply cannot be captured into words. In an instant, clarity washed over me, and I effortlessly started to translate my mental notes into written words. Was it some sort of supernatural power? No, I believe that the right moment has just come. And now, it's time to grasp the next crucial piece of the formula behind the bonus.

As we all know, money must be ensured by something. Traditionally, in the existing financial system, gold has been considered to be the best backing asset, but first of all, many countries, including America, have enacted laws allowing money printing without gold backing. Second of all, gold is a natural resource that also has volatility [changes in value], thus influencing the value of currencies backed by it. And lastly, gold can be devalued, as demand for it may decrease, and its value may align, for example, with the value of copper or other base metals.

I think there's no need to explain that the value is determined by market consumers. If they reduce their activity, the price decreases. In reality, a resource like gold can't be considered a full backing, not to mention we have never seen it, even when it was the official backing asset. Gold was stored in safes, banks, and state vaults, and we were only informed of its presence.

In our formula, as you may have guessed from the chapter title, the backing asset is time. I understand the perplexity of materialists—that is quite normal in the material world. We all, to a greater or lesser extent, are materialists, as we ourselves consist of matter. However, time cannot be touched, placed in a safe, borrowed or lent, especially not from the young to give to the elderly. Of course, not for the purpose of living longer—that belongs to the realm of other civilizations. But time is one of the most valuable resources given to us for lifelong ownership. It is stable and measurable; everyone possesses it equally from birth to death.

Time is Money

These words are not just an aphorism. They have practical significance, and this can be easily illustrated. Imagine a clock where, with every graceful sweep of the second hand, a golden ingot emerges from a magical portal. Would you like to have such a clock?

There is a statement that everything we desire is already with us, but we may not always see it. I'm talking about time. Every day, for millions of years, time counts the same number of minutes for our planet. The formula designed to heal the existing financial system transforms time into a material state. Bonuses appear in the public repository in accordance with time. This means that every day our shared time is converted into a material state. By engaging in our favorite activities, we can earn bonuses and precisely know how many of them there will be even in a thousand years.

What is more valuable: time or gold? Let's go step by step. The value of gold is determined by the market and is based on supply and demand. Gold is commonly considered a scarce commodity due to its limited natural abundance in the Earth's crust. I won't argue against that, but who knows exactly how many extraction sites there are for gold in the world? Who knows exactly how much gold is stored in each of the said extraction sites? Even geologists do not have precise information about it; they can only estimate the approximate number of these sites. Yet people are asked to believe that gold is a scarce commodity.

Now, let's consider a bonus backed by time. We know how many bonuses are born each day. In the public repository, you can see how many people are mining materialized time—Grand bonus or another bonus created by the formula. This means that by looking into the public repository, anyone can verify the demand for the bonus.

The market determines the value based on supply and demand. We, the people, create the market and everything handmade in the world. In the case of gold, the value is formed through information we have not verified, while in the case of the bonus, it is formed through information that is open and accessible to everyone. In addition to all this, we can see the average cost of mining at any given moment.

The cost of mining is measured not in terms of money, but in terms of time. As always, it's very easy. If there are, on average, one million miners in a day, it means they could each mine ten bonuses because there are ten million bonuses born each day. If the next day there are two million miners, then the cost of mining doubles, and over the same period, you can mine half as much, on average, five bonuses per person.

Of course, these are average figures since you obviously can't yield the same number of bonuses by wearing the bracelet during a walk and performing physical labor, for example, but the indicator is precise and is updated every minute. Remember the clock with ingots of gold, emerging from the magical portal? Well, it's real, but in our case, gold is a measurable asset in the form of a bonus that is valued accordingly. We can mine it and use it to buy goods and services, thereby strengthening the existing financial system.

Let me share a mystical incident that occurred to me in 2014. I was reviewing financial documents while sitting in a chair at the desk of a rented apartment in Moscow. Suddenly, an inexplicable and incomprehensible thought struck me: "What if we change the time format from twenty-four hours a day to ten?" That seemed to be nonsense, but still I pursued the idea.

In reality, a large part of the world has long been using the decimal system of measurement. Meters, liters, kilograms, and other units have become a successful replacement for feet, barrels, pounds and so on. But time remained in its old format. No one, as I thought at that moment, had tried to change it. Just to divide the day into ten parts —that's it!

Surprisingly, I learned from the internet that decimal time had, in fact, been introduced in France in 1793. Later, in 1795, it was canceled by the new politicians in power. To be honest, I wasn't particularly interested in all the formalities of what happened back then. What I was really focused on in that moment were the emotions and vibrations resonating throughout my body after receiving this information. I didn't even move when the wind blew the papers off my desk from the partially open window. I felt with my whole being that I needed this information, but I only understood its purpose eight years later. That's how it goes. The time came to reveal the formula for healing the existing financial system. I still don't care whether I discovered it myself, or someone else had done it long before me. What matters—is to convey the information. To let the world know that it exists.

So, we have learned that money belongs to us because we are a human resource that consumes and buys goods and services with money. We have also understood that the old system didn't take the existence of the human resource into account, and that's why the system itself is in a critical state now. However, it can be healed by gradually incorporating human resources into it. To do so, we introduce bonuses backed by time into the system.

Allow me to give you an example. As we know, there are twenty-four hours in a day. Not twenty-three or twenty-five. This means that time is a stable resource given to humanity for calculation. Each person has their own personal time from birth to death. And all of humanity has common time, which is twenty-four hours a day. The formula converts this communal time into bonuses to distribute them among us according to our daily activities.

When I tried to convey this information, financial "geniuses" were left speechless. I can easily understand them: the fear of change intensified when they realized the inevitable collapse of the system that was clear to them. Any further explanations about the formula were no longer appropriate.

During live broadcasts, I often mentioned my readiness to engage in debates with any scientist who could present at least one argument against backing currency with time. So far, I haven't managed to find such a scientist. My dear reader, I confirm my words and stand behind them: I am ready to conduct such debates; my account can be found on all social media platforms.

You may be wondering how the bonuses backed by time can be distributed among all people? How are the bonuses integrated into the existing system?

I am eager to answer all of your questions, but first I would like to explain how the Grand bonus is backed by time and how to find the exact proportion.

The formula divides a day into ten million equal parts and the Grand bonus is one part out of ten million. Since there are only twenty-four hours in a day, the number of bonuses cannot be less or more than ten million. That's where the decimal measurement system came in handy over time.

We talked about how to mine bonuses by doing what we love, for our benefit or for the benefit of humanity. To facilitate this, the Grand Time fund, created by us, integrates a bonus system into programs capable of measuring the quantity and quality of our actions to allocate bonuses. Additionally, thousands of existing programs with millions of users, working daily, will join the bonus system. We also understand that the bonus, being a healing remedy, will be gradually integrated into the economy. Rapid integration, on the other hand, might accelerate the destruction of the ailing system instead of healing it.

I believe you've noticed that I regularly repeat what has already been said in the previous chapters. I'll explain why: false information has passed down from generation to generation. It is so deeply rooted in people's minds that a long time is needed to absorb something new. However, we know about the remedy, and by applying it every day we can gradually heal the existing system.

This book is here to help unveil the secrets of the elixir and use it daily. Anyone who has read up to this point has already started to comprehend how the formula works. In the following chapters, we will learn how the new remedy will change the world in the spheres of medicine, education, and future technologies.

7

THE START OF THE FORMULA IMPLEMENTATION

What was the first thing I did? I shared how we can change the global financial system on social media platforms. Then I gathered people, conducted presentations... The website was up. It was running and gaining momentum very quickly. And what happened next?

I prematurely allowed myself to evaluate our honest currency. I wanted to show results to those who believed in my system, those who started this journey with me. From that very moment unpleasant situations began to occur. The software developers, on whom I spent over a million dollars, couldn't create a simple platform—not because they were foolish, and not because my qualifications did not allow for it —the Creator just did not allow me to take the next step.

While discussing how to modify our presentation without changing the strategy, Raf and I concluded that the Universe was guiding us again, preventing us from entering the funds of the old system with our new formula. Like in an old parable—the Universe was carrying us in its arms. No matter how firmly we pursued our own path, at every shareholder meeting, investors tried to sabotage all our efforts. Perhaps you are interested to know where we found the money for establishing the fund—not even one but, subsequently, funds in all regions—to support such a massive project as healing the global financial system. We'll get to that a bit later.

Let's get back to the book and what caused me to put all my thoughts on paper. Several factors prompted me to write it. To begin with, I couldn't convey my ideas to anyone. People perceived me as a dreamer, a scammer, an extraterrestrial or some other incomprehensible character that should be avoided to prevent catching crazy ideas. When I talked about the formula to people in the financial world, they used to interrupt me very quickly. No matter how well I expressed myself or where I started, it all ended in the first few minutes. The fear of change was stronger than reason. And when I tried to explain my idea to acquaintances, they listened out of respect, but I could still see their confusion and lack of understanding. If these were employees hired by me, I could observe the impatience on their faces: finish your speech faster, we have other things to do...

For almost six years, I had been beating my head against the wall of misunderstanding. I believed in the reality of my idea almost alone. Here, a clarification is necessary: alone in the business world. But there is another world that has been inspiring me all these years—my team. Despite my mistakes and failures, my people always remained by my side, ready to help, performing any and all tasks, sometimes even the ones that seemed unconquerable. And that is amazing to witness! It gives me strength to move forward and push skeptics aside.

My team is not accepted in the business world. They are often looked down upon and even called derogatory names, and that prevents me from being one of the representatives of a successful business in the existing ailing financial system. I have no desire to continue the conversation with people who say, "Oh, you have eighty thousand guinea pigs!" or "Oh, you have eighty thousand mouths waiting for profit." NO! "I have eighty thousand people who believe in my idea, and that is worth much more than the money you are afraid to invest." That is how I did not respond due to my character, and still I always said, "No, I have eighty thousand people who believe in my idea, and that is worth a lot." Usually, the conversation ended there. Yes, I do want to be one of them but in a new flourishing financial system that the formula is meant to heal.

The second factor is people who play a significant role in achieving the goal against their will. I have already mentioned some of them—those hired by me for work. Many, for personal reasons, could not find a job they liked, and consequently, they didn't care about the overall result. I had to part with such people, but eventually, a strong team was formed. As usual, not without the help of another failure.

When funding suddenly stopped and I had to announce it, I advised everyone to find jobs elsewhere and, if they wished, to obtain bonuses in their free time. The most valuable employees stayed with me, and a real team was formed. They focused on results. Such a team is worth paying for, and you can fully trust these people.

My family also found themselves hostages to the current situation. For many years it was very difficult for my loved ones to endure my failures. But they believed in me and hoped that everything would be fine soon. The sale of property, both movable and immovable; debts; loans; being followed; emigration; hard work... All this had to be experienced by those close to me, but they stayed by my side and believed in success. Partners, who invested money, also found themselves in a difficult situation. My son was among them. Despite all the inconveniences and hardships listed above, he stayed with me, and I am endlessly grateful to him. Another partner, my son's friend, decided to exit the project without waiting for results.

I don't blame people who leave. And, to be honest, I admit that I made fun of all the partners quite a bit. Only those devoted to the idea remained; those who didn't wait around but acted and achieved results with me. We're talking about a community having thousands of people. I call them partners, and at the moment, they are setting up Grand Time investment funds in their countries. After all the trials and unsuccessful attempts, we became one big team because our personal interests fully coincide with the ideological ones. Almost six years ago, we started to heal the global financial system together, investing our personal time and financial resources.

The formula is perceived easier and much quicker by ordinary people, those whose enrichment it was created for, and that is its advantage. Our fund is specifically created to finance various programs in all spheres of activity, capable of measuring the quantity and quality of actions. These programs will operate according to our concept, which is: "getting richer by giving away." In other words, with the help of these programs people from around the world will be able to get bonuses for their actions and use them as money.

What are we actually distributing, and how does the financial system recover in the process? Bonuses are deferred profits and the owner of the bonus is the owner of the deferred profit. Let's consider an example with a gaming platform. We play games and don't think about where the money comes from to create thousands of such platforms. In reality we all finance them. The platform, either secretly or openly, shows us ads and is paid for that by the advertiser. Additionally, we pay for subscriptions and other features, and this constitutes an overall multimillion capital for said platform, the result of which, in its term, funds the current financial system.

Now, let's take the example of the same gaming platform joining our bonus system. Here I want to draw your attention to the fact that each earned bonus belongs to the person who earned it. A gaming platform and any other organization joining the bonus system have no relation to the bonuses. The task of all such organizations is to provide the system with data on the quantity and quality of actions performed by people earning bonuses. Now back to the gaming platform that has joined the system. We obtain bonuses for all our actions, therefore, you get bonuses simply for the time spent in the game. The platform acquires new users—who wouldn't want to get bonuses for what they do in their free time? Consequently, the platform can now charge more from their advertisers and get deferred profit, while we, users, receive it in bonuses. When we accumulate a sufficient amount, we can use it to purchase goods and services we need. Playing games won't give you bonuses proportional to what you get for physical labor, of course, but it's still deferred profit, except you earned it in your free time.

There is a statement: "If a person is alone and no one sees them, that person doesn't exist; no one can confirm their existence." The same happens with gaming platforms: if no one plays, watches ads, or pays for their subscriptions, then those gaming platforms don't exist either.

A similar example can be drawn with pastries: there aren't any of them without buyers, nor are there factories that make them. If we don't exist, there are no houses, roads, power stations, or groceries in the stores. I hope that even the most experienced capitalist of the old system now understands that we, ordinary people, are the foundation of the entire financial system. We pay for everything and create everything handmade on the planet, and until now, this couldn't be properly calculated or appreciated.

Where do we get the money to distribute? To answer this question, I'll say: we are the money of the existing financial system. The old system couldn't evaluate the most important capital. It is systematically sawing off the branch it's sitting on. Poor politicians have to deceive us for the sake of maintaining "stability," printing new money, and participating in conflicts to distract our attention. It's truly pitiful when you realize the world of lies they have to exist in.

In the formula for healing the old financial system, the foundation is people and their personal bonuses that have not been valued until now. Modern technologies allow us to estimate the value of people's actions from birth to death. We earn bonuses by doing what we love: posting on social media, baking sweets, simply walking around, or sweeping the floor. The formula assesses our actions, based on complexity and time, after which it adds Grand to everyone's special personal wallet.

I hope that now it's clear where we get bonuses. But how are they distributed? It's even simpler: just buy goods and services with your bonuses. This function is provided in the bonus wallet. The system, in exchange for bonuses, provides goods and services, after which the bonus enters the general circulation of the financial system; it becomes valued and acquires the status of a vaccine for the recovery of said system. We will come back to this topic in other chapters, and it'll become clear why people will want to sell us goods and provide services for bonuses.

8

HOW THE BONUS WORKS

We have established a bonus rating system for all our actions. But before I start telling you about the remedy I found for all diseases, let me uncover the basic principles to follow on the path to a free existence, to a rich and happy life. In these matters, I will clearly state the facts.

Firstly, do not spend all your savings on buying bonuses that assess human resources. This is a huge mistake imposed on us by the existing system. Those who love profitable deals are especially at risk: funds, investors, traders, and other representatives of the financial system.

When we started earning bonuses almost six years ago, we faced the following situation: the bonus was listed on the exchanges and its value sharply increased, multiplying by hundreds in a couple of months, and then, naturally, plummeted. I will explain why. Unethical investors monitor the market, and when they see, for example, an asset worth one million nominal units, they start buying it without looking at the cost. Because of these purchases, the value of the asset begins to rise very quickly, and people who believe that the price will continue to rise fall into this trap. Then these deceitful investors sell all the purchased assets, but at an extremely high cost, since it grew due to onlookers who thought that they were lucky. Onlookers, on the contrary, hold on to their assets, as most often, they are precious to them or are their only savings. Such people naively believe that a miracle will happen and the price will go up again. This happens until they lose all the money they invested. This should not be done with an asset that has not yet strengthened. My dear liars, the new system will leave you pantless—I took care of it. This way we will only transfer the current deceitful strategy into a new economic model.

Secondly, do not rush to sell. Treat the bonus as an asset that provides more opportunities with each passing day. Buy goods and services, make profitable investments, and even if you withdraw, do it in the smallest amount possible. Selling diminishes the potential for multiplication, while buying gives this opportunity. Our task is to restrain the rapid growth of value, and we have all the necessary tools for doing that. These tools are understandable for everyone, and they are designed to facilitate advantageous storage, minimizing the desire to withdraw the bonus.

The bonus system is not meant for being placed on the stock exchange, but we realize that this will happen. Since we have experience with that, we are ready for such events to occur. The entire financial world understands that ultimately the market is the main evaluative mechanism in the existing system. It has been in place since ancient times and does not need changes.

Thirdly, I recommend to mine bonuses only in your free time, deliberately allocating a minimum of fifteen minutes a day for yourself and your passion. This is a psychological factor that, in addition to the opportunity to accumulate your bonus capital, allows you to realize your own value. Each of us is the entire global financial asset.

Differences in Bonus Systems

"Show me your friends, and I'll tell you who you are." This statement is relevant in every sense.

People undergo significant transformations after a change in their environment. Numerous examples of identical twins or even just friends after a long time of separation demonstrate this fact. Twins, initially indistinguishable, develop different characteristics after several years of separate lives: facial wrinkles, gestures, reactions to identical situations. Friends who haven't seen each other for a long time may note upon meeting how much they've changed and how incompatible their life principles have become—it doesn't matter that they were like two peas in a pod in their childhood. This indicates that in choosing a society for ourselves we gradually become a part of it. And society, in turn, assimilates a small piece of our individuality.

The same principle works when we choose the bonus system. To make the right choice, it is necessary to understand the fundamental differences between all bonus systems.

Bonus systems exist in various fields. Many airlines give bonuses when we purchase tickets—by accumulating them one can obtain a "free" ticket. Banks, stores, gaming applications, and even workplaces provide bonuses for our actions. However, the fundamental difference between all these bonus systems lies in the fact that they are an integral part of the existing financial system. In reality, we don't earn them; we receive them as rewards. At work, if we perform specific tasks, we are rewarded with bonuses. If we purchase goods in a store for a certain amount, we receive a discount or an opportunity for the next "free purchase." Thus, all current and future reward systems, created outside the formula's conditions, operate like conventional money. They hinder the healing of the existing financial system, and by staying in it, we keep our old way of thinking. Remember: "Show me your friends, and I'll tell you who you are."

I can break that apart using any example, but the fact remains: to cover all types of rewards, companies need money. In other words, if these are airline tickets, one needs to finance the aircraft fuel, pilots' salaries, and other expenses. If a social network distributes bonuses, its users receive them from the budget of the same financial system. And even if a high-end clothing store collaborates with a social media platform, an airline, and a chain of cafes, creating a unified bonus system with a public database and bonus accumulation, it won't adhere to the formula, as the essence of this alliance bears a commercial interest for individual stores, airlines, social networks, and cafes. This replicates the existing model of the outdated financial system.

A bonus program based on a formula implies absolute ownership by us. We decide in which areas of activity to apply it.

The essence of the formula can be illustrated by swimming in a pool. In the first case, you swim for money. In the second, created by the formula, you swim because you want to do it and, at the same time, you obtain bonuses. The difference is significant but we often don't notice it, as we view everything through the prism of the system, considering it normal to act against our own desires.

In the old system we earn bonuses in the form of money printed on machines; in this case, we don't change our worldview. By earning bonuses according to the formula, we change ourselves and help each other change. The saying works both ways. "Show me your friends, and I'll tell you who you are."

When airlines, stores, cafes, and social media platforms join our public bonus system, they will have to be the best in order for us to choose them. Just like swimming in a pool for our pleasure. And when we join their bonus system, we swim against our desires. The choice is ours.

Similar bonus systems can emerge at the state level, in non-profit, public, religious and other organizations. Their goal is also to attract public resources without considering the true value of human assets. It's important for us to not only understand this fact but also to think about it constantly, always keeping it in our minds. Yet, we have been hardwired to think differently. We are accustomed to forgetting our own value and giving our strength and time to a system that temporarily allows us to use our assets.

In a system that operates according to the formula, we choose where we want to spend our time. We apply efforts into fulfilling our desires. In such conditions, we can achieve significantly more results and develop in different spheres. When one person makes progress in a certain area, the whole society does so because each of us is a representative of our society.

In future generations, bonus systems created by the formula will completely transform into a coherent mathematical model that does not need correction. They will autonomously develop in public databases without the possibility of external influence. Brilliant programmers like Vitalik Buterin[1] are already testing and implementing such functionality. This will give financial specialists the ability to predict the growth of bonus systems without errors for decades ahead. It will mean that the estimation of the value of human resource has become the foundation of the financial system and all people are wealthy from birth.

---

[1] Vitalik Buterin (born January 31, 1994) is a Canadian programmer; co-founder and former editor of Bitcoin Magazine; co-founder of the Ethereum project.

2

PEOPLE-RETIREES

While communicating with people about various topics, I often heard the phrase, "I want to earn enough money to do nothing." When I asked why they wanted this, the responses included people saying that they would start traveling the world, doing what they love and so on. At that point I would say, "You've just mentioned that you want to do nothing, but you've listed a dozen things." We have already discussed this topic in the chapter on getting rid of lies. People lie to themselves; the substitution of concepts happens at a subconscious level. We may not even realize what we truly want. If we dig deeper and ask, "Why do you want to travel?" the answers will reveal more imbalances.

"I want to live in hotels that always have clean bedding and towels. I want to dine in expensive restaurants, get massages and other rejuvenating procedures..." It turns out that people confuse the notions of "travel" and "comfort." They want ordinary comfort and, for some reason, plan to go somewhere for it. But traveling is not always comfortable; people travel to see the world with their own eyes, feel the heat of a desert, climb Mount Everest, immerse themselves in another culture, and interact with different people... Certainly not just for a massage which is cheaper to get at the nearest salon.

We've already discussed the influence of the formula on the substitution of concepts. In this chapter, we need to understand how humanity will feel living in complete comfort and well-being. I started with the substitution of concepts to dispel the myth imposed on us by the existing system. It sounds something like this: if everyone is rich, then no one will want to work. Yes, this could happen if it occurred overnight, but not because people don't want to work. It's because they no longer want to be enslaved by money. More precisely, they don't want to be slaves to the established reality that oppresses ordinary people, driving them into dependency.

The formula allows us to gradually move away from slave-like dependence, engage in our favorite activities, and obtain bonuses. This way, we find our true purpose and gain energy for self-realization. Through a smooth redistribution, employees of different spheres will switch places, and each person will be able to pursue their passion. Yes, it's easy!

No person on the planet, unless confined to a bed, can willingly lie on the couch for an extended period. People in prisons and hospitals understand this concept very well. Finding pleasure and lying on the couch for a month are entirely different things. For example, lying on the couch and watching a show is an action for which you can obtain bonuses—though much less than for physical labor. Even walking can bring bonuses. We will accumulate them for almost all actions that contribute to the well-being of society as well as ours.

If the question of who will pay for this still bothers you, I advise you to reread the book. It's normal. For centuries, we have been told that we owe something to someone, but this concept is wrong. We, the ordinary people, are the foundation of the entire global financial system, and by engaging in our favorite activities, we elevate the standard of living. We will invent more, implement new technologies faster and better, and truly value everyone, quite literally, in a digital sense. This is already possible thanks to the formula. Don't be surprised if we start to take inspiration from those sweeping our neighborhood territories—they do it for their own pleasure.

People of ordinary professions, who make the world more comfortable to live in, can become the idols of our time. A builder who doesn't need money will construct for the convenience and comfort of others. A janitor with a full account balance will sweep to make the world cleaner. A doctor will do everything to keep people healthy and, accordingly, will prevent diseases rather than treat them. A biologist will take care of people's healthy nutrition... Everyone will engage in their favorite activities.

We weren't brought here to make money by deceiving each other and, ultimately, ourselves. Let's devote our lives to a true purpose! Let's give birth to children, build houses, create clean and comfortable environments at home—all while obtaining bonuses and becoming richer.

By the way, in our community there's a group where stay at home moms receive bonuses for cleaning their own houses. This process of cleaning is necessary for the whole family, but until now it has not been considered "work." In fact, even physically strong people find it difficult to clean the house. The benefits of such an activity are well-known: a clean home fosters comfort and leads to people wanting to spend more time there—relaxing and communicating with their families. We leave for work and return to a clean house with great pleasure. Stay at home moms contribute to healing the existing financial system not only directly, by obtaining bonuses, but also indirectly, by enhancing the education and productivity of all family members.

While in school, one of our project participants had a dream of writing a book. But as life moved closer to the age of retirement, that dream got lost in everyday hustle, chasing after money that always seemed to be in short supply.

After joining the project, this participant was offered to write a book for bonuses in her free time: with no deadlines, no obligations, and no need for text approval, just as her soul desired. As a result, the book was published, the dream came true and the bonuses were obtained. That is how the new time will work and that's just a fact! Now the book "Notes of PRO* Rebels and Dreamers" by Olga Lu can be found on all online platforms if you want to purchase it and give it a read.

The substitution of concepts has become so ingrained in our lives that even at a young age, we dream of earning enough money to "do nothing," to retire with our own capital. However, when the retirement age comes, we want to be in demand, to create something, and usually we have enough strength and energy for all that. In the new reality, the concept of "retirement" simply won't exist. All people, from birth to death, will be able to obtain bonuses by engaging in their favorite activities. Since every individual is valuable at any age, company leaders won't need to force people into retirement. If they are doing what they love, they will achieve better results than any young and inexperienced "specialist". And if they want, they can master a new profession at the age of ninety—all while obtaining their own bonuses and strengthening the financial system. This is what we observe in our community:

"I worked in leadership positions for a long time. After retirement, my life changed significantly. The leadership qualities I possess were unnecessary without my beloved job. I can't say it was boring; I was raising grandchildren, helping my children, and engaging in community work. But I knew I could do more. I spent all my free time looking for interesting ideas on social media. When I saw Artur in a live broadcast and was able to ask him a few questions, I immediately understood—this is for me. The Grand Time project surpassed all my expectations in terms of the scale of its idea, and my life has taken on new colors even more than before. I am grateful to the Universe for the chance to be at the forefront of healing the global financial system. The project allows me to use my leadership qualities for the good. It's awesome!" These are the words of our participant Galia Moon.

This example and others, that can be seen among the reviews of our foundation, show that by receiving formula bonuses and doing what we love in our free time, we open up new opportunities, new skills, new knowledge and find new sources for development at any age. The formula works for absolutely everyone.

10

EDUCATION IS THE FOUNDATION OF A SOCIETY CONSISTING OF INTEREST-BASED COMMUNITIES

Remember I mentioned that I don't have academic degrees in finance? That's indeed true. Despite studying at the Economics Faculty of the Rostov State University of Railway Communications, practical knowledge has always been more valuable to me than theoretical. Even if I were to defend a doctoral dissertation, I would still consider myself a practical expert. I would be glad to have specialized doctors as co-authors in the technical documentations of the fund. It will be very interesting and detailed work.

Every field of science undergoes changes. This happens because people constantly add new facts and discoveries. To stay on top of everything, you need to be immersed in the field. This is why I didn't mention my Ph.D. in Economics, as I consider practical knowledge more important than theoretical.

We start learning from birth. We come into this world ready to accept and process new knowledge. We absorb information with mother's milk and study everything around us. It's one of the functions ingrained in humans by nature. First and foremost, we demand attention: we cry when it's cold and get warmed up; we cry when we are hungry and get fed... Then we learn to walk and talk, continuously studying the world around us.

The ability to learn is a natural gift given at birth. We can use it throughout our lives by learning everything that interests us. But when we are small, the world, in the form of our mothers, takes care of us. Having no fear, we don't limit ourselves during the process of learning.

Imagine the shock of a child, used to kindness, when suddenly his beloved mother shouts, "Stop, that's a socket, you could get shocked! Careful, there's a table corner, don't get hurt! Stop, there's fire, don't burn yourself!" What happens in this situation? The child faces fear and is afraid to do anything, including learning, without the approval of an adult.

Just imagine the heights in learning we could achieve without fear! Without interrupting the natural learning process given to us by nature, we can learn throughout life and experience the excitement that can be compared to taking our first steps.

What happens to us when we are told that now, all of a sudden, we have to learn? First at school, then at a university. Many of us do not see the point in this. A protest against the system is a normal reaction. Why should I study? Who do I owe that to?

I remember myself at that age. I also remember explaining to Raf how I dealt with it. He asked Kristina and I a question: "What do I need all these sciences for? Maybe I'll choose a profession that has nothing to do with them."

Kristina has a strong sense of duty—she graduated from school with a gold medal and university with a red diploma (meaning she had straight As her whole life)—so she was determined in this matter. But I understood my son very well: I myself don't agree with being forced to do things I don't want to do. In this world, unfortunately, people often do what they have to, not what they want to. I explained to a seven-year-old child that there are generally accepted rules that cannot be changed and that he won't even get a job without secondary education. In short, I was talking nonsense. I had to persuade and convince my son to sacrifice his childhood for some universally accepted rules.

Raf met us halfway—he even entered the medical field and studied for two years there. Simultaneously he started his own business. One day he came to me hoping I would understand him if he left university. I happily gave him that opportunity, and since then, Raf has been following his own path, not the one his parents chose for him. By the way, we had imposed the medical field on him as an alternative to musical education, which he was more inclined towards.

Unfortunately, parents with such upbringing often prepare their children for being slaves to the existing financial system. At that time, I wasn't an exception.

Let's imagine how the educational system will be arranged in a society where everyone is wealthy and each person has a choice of where to live and what to do. From the moment of birth, people will be obtaining bonuses and will be able to choose their life path independently. The choice doesn't necessarily have to be made at a certain age. In a world where every person is valuable, making mistakes is not scary; you can safely change your path if that's what you want.

Bonuses are also awarded for mistakes made while learning. In such a world, independent learning processes never stop. The interest in gaining knowledge never ceases, it's just done on an individual level. We explore the world through conversations with interesting people, through reading and studying science, through our mistakes and difficulties. Everyone comes to the realization of purpose and moves towards it intuitively in their own way and on their own time.

The main task of parents and society is to support children and create comfortable conditions for their education. My daughter Olya, in this regard, followed Kristina's interest in sciences and was always encouraged by us. Even now, in her third year of studying at a university, she knows that she will continue her studies and defend her Ph.D. This suggests that each child is individual, despite the fact that they were born from the same parents and grew up in the same environment.

Any parent wants to shield their children from difficulties and guide them to the right path, but is that really the child's path? We often forget that children have their own, unique way in life.

How will those that are aware study? In the current world, we observe common trend of people forming different communities. There are groups based on religious, scientific, political and many other interests in the material world, and these groups are often created on social media. I remember the day when Raf and I arrived in Silicon Valley—it was a refreshing change. I recognize the value of surrounding oneself with like-minded souls. That is how growth happens, where wings sprout, and new knowledge blossoms. From a young age, we begin to explore the world, and the gained knowledge multiplies when children enter a community of people who share their interests. That is exactly how entire cities of like-minded people will be formed. There won't be any obstacles such as struggling to find where to live and how to pay for a place in a new society.

How will the formula for healing the existing financial system affect this process? The magic begins with getting our own bonuses. By obtaining them, we start to value ourselves. This happens for two reasons: first, we dedicate time to ourselves by doing what we love, and second, we get bonuses for our favorite activities, gradually forming our capital.

People who understand their value, look at the world differently, taking responsibility for everything happening around them. When the awareness of responsibility comes, we won't walk past a piece of paper thrown on the ground next to the trash can. Our participation, even in such seemingly insignificant matters, will feel necessary. We begin to realize that everything in the material world is paid for with our human resources. I deliberately remind you of the fact that there are no roads, buildings, or electricity without us. We are the foundation of the

44

existing system. When we begin to appreciate our value, the healing process of the system starts to take place.

Now let's go back to communities created for learning or exploring things that interest us. Do you like biology? That's great! Thousands of other people are also passionate about it; they have joined a large community where cities with laboratories and all the necessary infrastructures have been built for them. Can you imagine the efficiency of such a community? Local television channels will report daily on new discoveries. Everything—from mass media to friends, acquaintances, and neighbors—will have the same interests. People will be graduating from the university called "life." Creating a family with someone who shares your interests is also cool: there will always be common topics for discussion.

Do you like building spaceships? There will be a community for that too, and you will be welcomed there because you are a person! And as previously discussed, a person is the most valuable resource in the material world. If you are still in the process of self-discovery, you can change communities until you find your own path. Creating communities based on interests is the most progressive form of education that will provide significant development for society—even if we come to this after several generations pass by.

At the beginning of the book I touched upon the topic of authorities in the new society. Allow me to repeat this idea: people with big wallets won't necessarily have prestige in the new society. Now you can imagine what kind of importance plumbers, for instance, will feel in a city created for biological scientists. They will be highly valued, as scientists typically don't even know which way a faucet should be turned, let alone where the pipes for water supply are located. While engaging in what they love, plumbers will be able to choose the cities and communities where they feel comfortable making this world more convenient for everyone. Each of us is different.

11

POLITICS

In the previous chapters, I mentioned that politicians are unable to change the existing system. They understand the irreversibility of destruction better than anyone else and are forced to seek ways to preserve everything as it is, at least for some time.

I've heard many stories about my grandfather Ovanes, my mother's father. Even after moving to Chicago, I met a man at the gym who happened to know my grandfather and was eager to tell me a few facts about him. Although all the stories I heard were different, they always ended up the same way. Everyone would make sure to say how much of a kind-hearted man my grandfather was. I knew that. I saw it myself. He always treated me with great care, and I loved him deeply.

When my grandfather died, different people, from the former mayor of the city to warehouse employees, all spoke about his kindness. He was a simple man and very heartfelt, which is quite rare in our time. But if such a person were the president of the country, he wouldn't be able to change the system. Alas, presidents are also hostages of it.

Allow me to explain. To achieve such a result, all presidents must come to an agreement, but how is that supposed to happen when there are still constant fights and debates over borders, exchange rates, global dominance... Should I go on?

What lies behind these disagreements? Money—that's right. Money that will be spent on weapons. That is the reality of the current system. By the way, we are also the ones paying for it, therefore indirectly becoming accomplices in armed conflicts.

There is a belief that if all people suddenly refuse to pick up weapons, there will be no more wars. Yes, that would work, but people aren't going to magically wake up ready to go against the system overnight. Even if it did happen, such sudden changes would disrupt the system rather than heal it. The good news, however, is that we are already aware individuals—we just need time to change the world. This time will pass as an instant for the Universe, while for us it might take several generations. Each person can experience this awakening from the moment of personal realization. When we begin to obtain bonuses, the system will start evaluating and truly valuing our actions. As a result, people will change their thinking and stop producing or using weapons.

In any, even the most democratic elections, we cast our votes, hoping that a particular person will make our lives better. Unfortunately, we don't change anything: the financial system remains the same, and every subsequent president becomes its hostage and is forced to produce weapons, expand the army, and so on. Money is needed for this, and we are the ones paying it. If we don't exist, then neither do countries, armies, weapons, nor borders.

The assessed human resource will gradually change our thinking; we will begin to value ourselves, and, accordingly, others will begin to value us too. This doesn't mean that politicians will hear our voices and do as we want. It's just that their consciousness will heal from years worth of lies, as will ours.

People don't need borders; people need freedom of action, freedom of movement. Any person should be able to live where they like. After the complete healing of the financial system, there will be no need to fight wars for borders, as the "wars" will be happening over the human resource, which is the foundation of the healed financial system. These "wars" will be aimed at making life better and more comfortable for ordinary people. Presidents are also people, just like you and me; they are supposed to serve us and make our lives more comfortable. A healthy financial system will help them in this.

What lies am I talking about?

For example, a so-called country, let's call it "A", is facing inflation and rising costs of essential food products, unable to stop this increase due to market competition within the existing system. The population of the country expresses dissatisfaction, leading to tension. In this case, there are several possible ways the problem could further develop.

Firstly, people might protest, go on strikes, and leave their jobs. This turn of events could have terrible consequences, even if it only lasts a few days. Transportation, hospitals, schools, police departments, stores, and other essential services may lack workers who have taken off to participate in these strikes.

The second way things could go is the most favored and common—to divert the population's attention. Mass media is used to distract us from pressing issues with alarming news. For instance, all channels may show impending natural disasters, incidents in neighboring countries, or the suppression of uprisings in country "B". Lastly, there could be an internal conflict arising from election results

47

that would be broadcasted and described in all its details. What can one say about food prices when the country is in such a difficult situation?

The third way is to print more money which would push the economy into an even more critical state, calming social tension for a short period. And then the cycle repeats. Who would still argue that politicians are not hostages of a rapidly declining financial system?

Let's refresh our memory. Both politicians and us are slaves to the existing financial system. The system is so vulnerable and outdated that it has to be kept from collapsing by all means, including interstate conflicts and other instruments that sustain its breakdown.

I think politicians, when alone with themselves, justify their actions with the only argument available to them. Fewer people die in conflicts than when compared to the hunger and chaos that would arise during the collapse of a financial system. But this can be resolved in a simple and understandable way—by injecting a fundamentally strengthening currency into the economy in the form of bonuses which are essentially deferred profits. As we know, bonuses are obtained through our actions, backed by the time and quality of these actions. By injecting bonuses into the system, we strengthen the existing currency, eliminating the need of printing extra money.

How does this happen?

I understand that this may seem unrealistic. Our brains struggle to accept the truth. But we are changing and realizing that we live in a world of lies, and this cannot last forever. It's time to heal the existing system.

You and I are injecting our financial capital into the economy in the form of a bonus. National currencies gradually start to strengthen without printing presses. There is no need to create projects for reforming the system. We know what any reforms lead to: first, the old is destroyed; second, the so-called "reform" begins to take effect. In our case, people themselves inject capital and strengthen the system. Capital, as we have already understood, is the properly assessed human resource. We are the most valuable investment. We are the only investment. There is no economy without us.

It's all very simple; you just have to believe in it. This belief is in yourself! Believe that you are the most valuable material creation on this planet. You are a human—the creator of all things handmade. You can change the situation by engaging in something you love, something that brings you satisfaction.

The path to prosperity for future generations begins here and now.

12

FEARS AND THEIR NATURE

Shame, debt, guilt, fear of change... Where do these feelings come from? Looks like another trick of the system. What do people do when they feel shame or guilt? These emotions usually evoke self-criticism. But what do we feel during this process?

Shame, debt, guilt. In fact, these words invoke fear, imposed by the system to control our subconscious. They have become so ingrained in our lives that they are even used in raising children. When children hear that they are guilty of something, they don't feel a sense of guilt; they are afraid of punishment. Later, an adult asks them if they are ashamed with a very serious expression on their face, when in reality, a child can't know what "shame" feels like. They realize that they need to agree, or else they will be punished. This is how we condition our children to obey the system, teaching them the key words to react to. They get old enough to go to school, and by that time the emotion of fear is automatically produced after hearing such words as "shame" or "guilt".

There shouldn't be a concept of shame at all. What is shame? This negative emotion arises only when our actions don't align with widely accepted norms. In other words, we owe something to someone. Someone invented norms by which we are supposed to live. But what if we have individual norms? Then we are shamed. That is absolutely absurd!

Every person has an immense value. Each of us contributes to the development of society, regardless of what we wear, how we look, or how we express our individuality.

There are norms and rules in every community. People accept them and live by these rules—that's normal, and it should be that way. However, if people do not conform to the rules of the community, it's natural that they don't want to be a part of it. What does shame have to do with all this? Those people chose to be different, and they should be able to find a community of like-minded individuals without feeling ashamed. Of course, you might say that if one wants to feel free, money is needed. It is the privilege of the rich—to be where you like. But that is the essence of the book.

When we are all wealthy enough, the feelings imposed on us by the old financial system will disappear, and only the genuine feelings, given to us by nature, will remain.

The sense of guilt is another concept that we invented and carried from ancient times, just like the feelings of duty to the homeland, society, or specific individuals, which are also imposed by the system.

In general, a person has two emotions from birth: fear and joy. There are hundreds of words conveying different forms of these two types of emotions, but fundamentally there are two of them.

You might get the impression that all this is impossible to prove. But it's easy. Children cry when they are scared and hungry. They cry when they see bright light or hear a loud sound—this is a natural animal instinct for self-preservation. In all other situations, they laugh and explore the world. If a child isn't taught to fear people or animals, they might play with them out of interest and learn from that, even with venomous snakes.

How can you feel shame if you don't know about it? Let's imagine that suddenly you wake up in a parallel world, surrounded by the same people, walking the same streets, but everyone is looking at you with interest. Then you notice that you don't have a tail, while others do. What feeling would arise in you in this situation? I dare to assume that your feelings would be based on people's reactions. If they bow to you, saying that you are a special person from the future, you would feel pride—that's a feeling similar to joy. If they avoid you while expressing disgust, your feelings would be related to fear. Insecurity and shame would cultivate the desire to grow a tail or find a society where everyone is tailless like you.

If you are rich, you would try to find your community. In addition, you would find fellow travelers, like-minded people exploring parallel worlds. And you wouldn't feel ashamed because your fellow travelers would value you for your unique qualities. They're not with you for money; they also want to find another world. This example shows how strongly we are influenced by society. The foundation has not been laid by nature, but by society itself since ancient times, and it has been supported by the system to this day.

Fear of change

Fear of change, like all types of fears, helps the system control people. Let's figure out under what circumstances it appears. When we don't know what lies ahead, the unknown scares us. That is, we are afraid of what has not yet happened but may happen. There are people among us who are ready for change. As a rule, these people have not lost interest in life; they take change as a given. But most people are afraid of change. They have the same routine day after day, week after week, year after year. Their entire lives can be compared to one storyline that's been on repeat thousands of times.

I've lived almost fifty years, to be precise, eighteen thousand and ninety four days. There have been many events in my life, and I have much to remember! Every day is unpredictable; we do not know what will happen even a minute from now. But we are given the opportunity to live, to accept changes and to rejoice in each day lived. We have imagination—on the one hand, it helps us embody ideas and moves us forward, while on the other hand, it hinders our development. Haven't you forgotten, my dear reader? You are part of humanity, and your development is the development of humanity.

Every person, consciously or subconsciously, analyzes the past. But nature doesn't count years. It counts days, and each new day is full of events, even for people who are afraid of changes.

By grouping three hundred and sixty five lived days into a year, we accordingly diminish the significance of one singular day—a day in which countless events of enormous importance occurred. I woke up in the morning, but it might not have happened. Therefore, a new day is a great event.

My day is scheduled by the minute in my daily planner; each task I've planned is an event. Do you suggest cramming all that into a three hundred and sixty five-day calendar? No! Every lived moment is essential for us, and the formula grants us bonuses precisely because each minute is important. After all, you and I are the most valuable resource on this planet. We are human.

Having outdated rules, the system dictates conditions that make it easier to sit and do nothing to avoid trouble. From the age of two, we are "protected" from dangers. "Don't touch the fire! Don't go outside!" Attempting to shield children, adults program them to fear. Consequently, the fear of change is imposed by the system.

The existing system benefits when it prevents us from thinking about moving to another country, where life might be better and more comfortable. Even without considering the formula, human resources remain the most crucial component. We pay for everything. But it's easier for the system to keep us from moving by instilling the fear of change than by creating comfortable conditions.

Changing your citizenship, place of residence and employment, marital status, or overall lifestyle—all of these things instill immense fear for one single reason: the lack of money.

If you have enough money, comfortable conditions will be created for you in any country. If you don't like your job, you'll change it without fear. Families will be strong not because of dependence on each other but due to their own beliefs. Changes won't be frightening; they will be enlightening.

The formula transforms our perception of change. By obtaining bonuses, we gradually open up possibilities and begin to value every minute lived. After all, it's our choice.

But what about the fear of death?

The word "death" is a frightening word embodying the fear of many generations. In ancient times, losing the head of the family, often the provider returning from hunting, was a terrifying prospect. If a child, per say, got eaten by wild animals, the harsh reality was that it was seen as a form of natural selection. Though it may sound cynical, acknowledging these horrible truths is essential.

In emergency situations, we reveal our true feelings and desires. Ask yourself a question and try to answer it honestly. Whose life is more important: yours or your child's? You can answer this question if you've been in a situation where you had to make a choice. I personally had two vivid episodes that helped me to understand this point. In the past, I would have said that my life is more important to me and in an emergency, the instinct for self-preservation would kick in, and I would save myself. I still say this to my children, but they have the right not to believe me.

In the first case, Raf was just over a year old, barely starting to take his first steps, and everyone was protecting him from falls. Once, we were all standing in the kitchen and watching as his grandfather (a man with a doctorate) screwed a portable gas cylinder into a lamp. Suddenly, this fist-sized metal cylinder broke free and started flying all over, hitting the ceiling, the floor and everything in between. In such situations, instincts usually work, not brains. The fear of death was stronger than anything else. Raf's closest relatives forgot about him as they were all trying to save themselves. Perhaps, they saw that I shielded my son. Later I teased them, remembering that incident.

The second case was a car accident. After the crash, the car was totaled beyond repair. I covered Raf and Kristina, who was carrying Olya under her heart, with my body. Now you see that I answered the question untruthfully, not realizing how I would behave in an emergency. Now I know the right answer.

The fear of death is necessary for preserving the physical body. We need the body to fulfill our mission. Sometimes the death of a person serves as a life lesson to other people. A vivid example is the death of Jesus. In reality, death usually shocks those around us; it does not pass without a trace and always teaches something.

I was fortunate to see six of my great-grandparents alive and healthy but, on the other hand, I lost them at an early age, and I remember how deeply I experienced the fear of death. My relatives grieved. The words spoken in tears were especially memorable. Years later, when I lost many friends, I heard the same phrases from their relatives. I understood that we mourn and grieve for our loss. We realize that their body can no longer feel. Those who believe in God, wish peace to the soul, but all the suffering and grief are directed towards us. Phrases like "How will I live without you? Whom have you left me for?" directly speak about this. At the same time we feel sorry for the people who died. They deserved more! They could have lived longer!

Again we face the substitution of concepts: do we feel sorry for the person or for ourselves? As you can see, this substitution exists even in the most intimate and sensitive emotions. The roots of it are laid by the existing system since we had to be governed so that we could live in communities and survive to this day. Our reaction to words had to be submissive. As you see, fear is a feeling ingrained in a person from birth. It teaches survival and helps to preserve the physical body protecting it from various injuries. But around the feeling of fear, there are hundreds of words invented for manipulation through the usual natural fear of death, given to us for survival.

My attitude toward death has changed several times throughout my life. In early childhood, I thought about death with horror. I didn't want to lose my parents or grandparents. I was the firstborn, rather spoiled, and my relatives often argued whose turn it was to entertain me. I loved them all. When they asked me which grandmother I wanted to visit, it was difficult to decide—I was eager to be with both at once, but that was impossible. As a side note, I am grateful to my parents for this: from an early age, I was taught to make decisions independently, even through tears.

When I found out that people die, it was a shock to me. I was not ready to lose my loved ones. During my years of youthful maximalism, I was constantly tormented by the question: what was the point of giving birth to me? I considered myself a useless consumer and even voiced this complaint to my parents when the conversation turned to my dissolute lifestyle. "Did you ask for my permission when you were planning on having me?" One day, my mom asked me to write all my feelings down in a poem. Never before or after have I written poetry.

Here's what came out:

1. I'm afraid to tell you
2. What's going on in my head.
3. I can feel the filthy rats
4. Crawling by my hair strands.

After that "masterpiece," my relatives never asked me to write poetry again. My "creativity" made a profound impression on the readers.

I didn't want to live; I constantly played with death. I started smoking in front of my parents at the age of thirteen; then moved on to drugs and reckless driving... I danced on the edge of death numerous times. Not long ago, someone suggested creating a natal chart based on my birthdate, and I asked: "Which day should we take as a reference point?" Should we consider the day I died and was brought back to life as my birthday? The day when I was reborn...

I went through other periods at that age. For example, when my classmate and I opened our shoe workshop. I was fourteen when I started my first business. At that point, it felt like life had a purpose, and I wasn't worthless at all. However, it lasted only for three months, until I experienced my first bankruptcy.

I vividly remember my emotions. Initially, it was euphoric: we created jobs for three workers—our other classmates—and they earned well during the summer. Then disappointment came: the dream that everyone would wear the shoes, which we assembled from blanks, was shattered at the point of sale. We were not prepared to compete with other manufacturers for the place on the shelves of stores.

The teenage breaking point and the reluctance to live continued with even greater force. Naturally, at that time I didn't understand that all this was necessary for my experience, and I perceived every failure as my own incompetence.

After analyzing my bright and eventful life, I came to the conclusion that the desire to live awakened in me when I was needed. Most likely, my parents understood this, and when it was really difficult to hold me back, they resorted to the only correct solution: they asked me to help them. I found a job. I didn't have the strength and time for any nonsense. Although I realized that they could manage without me, I felt needed. And I was not afraid of death any more.

When my son was born, I clearly understood that I had no right to die. I remember it very well: I was flying on an airplane. I loved flying in bad weather and going through turbulence. When the plane started to jolt, I was delighted. I experienced the same excitement I did on rollercoasters when I was a kid. But not at that moment—my son was waiting for me, and I definitely had to come back.

The children grew up, but I found a purpose to live for. It was set on the day of my acquaintance with God when I expressed my disagreement with the existing system and shouted through anger that it shouldn't be this way. Money should serve people, and everyone should be provided with all necessary things for a comfortable life.

When you find a purpose, the fear of death disappears, and the feeling of having to fulfill the goal you have set appears. That is a marvelous feeling that fuels you with colossal energy to move forward —to pass on the knowledge you accumulated in life for the benefit of others.

After the release of this book, there will be enough information to implement the formula in various aspects of life. Even after I am gone. To die with a sense of duty fulfilled while understanding the profound benefits left behind, is worthy of the highest reward for a mission accomplished in this material world. And in the immaterial one, life is just starting.

Of course, I'm not saying goodbye. I have many plans for a step by step implementation of the formula and financing new projects designed to take into account the quantity and quality of actions for accumulating bonuses. I want to see more happy people living a rich and meaningful life.

13

HOW THE FORMULA WILL FREE US FROM FEAR

What does the formula have to do with improving the world's financial system? How will it help us get rid of fear?

I believe the reader has understood that the formula is directly related to self-realization. By receiving bonuses for any actions, one can strive for self-improvement in search of purpose. Reading books and obtaining bonuses, learning and obtaining bonuses, mastering professions and obtaining bonuses... Ultimately, by accumulating bonuses from birth, each of us will think about our desires rather than the need for food and shelter. Parents won't force their children to get education for the sake of a well-paying job, instead they will help their children find their real passion and excel in it.

But let's return to the topic of this chapter. Fear is an instinct inherent even in animals. Trainers tame tigers, using fear. A tiger, capable of neutralizing any trainer in one move, submits. Being rational beings, we recognized this and submitted to strong leaders under the influence of the fear of death. It was necessary for the evolution process, for the creation of communities, for protection against attacks, for discipline. Centuries later, we became conscious individuals, still dominated by fear. When we are hundreds of miles away from ongoing incidents, the truth is, there is nothing threatening us and there is nothing to fear. But wars, diseases, catastrophes, terrorism, accidents, and crashes haunt us every day. And even if we are far away from the source, receiving negative information still reminds us of the fear of death.

This book is not meant to blame politicians and the media, as you and I are both politicians and representatives of the media. All these people are among us; they are just like us, and they are also hostages to a false, malfunctioning financial system which is not able to resist pressure. People with less wealth are affected to a lesser extent, while people with more wealth and those close to the authorities are affected more. Accusations won't help figure it out, let alone help correct the current situation. Only a universal reassessment and a transition to a new stage of evolutionary development can help. And as I have already written, this stage has arrived: we are already using the formula that leads us to this very reassessment.

Review from Jeannette who lives in Spain comes in quite fittingly: "I married a Spaniard. For many years, I missed not only my relatives but also my life in my home country, to which I was very attached. My family, friends, and my environment have always been important to me. In Spain, same as in Europe, people plan their lives, and there's no time for boredom. Both my husband and his family love me very much. But I can't say that I was completely happy. I was haunted by a feeling of fear for my family. It seemed that something bad might happen to them, and I would not be able to be there, since I was very far away. And then I became part of a massive experiment to improve the world's financial system! Now I understand that all fears were created by my sad experiences and, in fact, there is no point in being afraid of what is not there. Now I am in the spotlight; I receive tremendous energy from participating in the project every day, and I live a full life again. All my loved ones are with me, and we are no longer discussing how scary it is to be far away from each other, but how we have united with the help of an idea and no longer feel the distance between countries. I realized that the idea is capable of working wonders, and they began happening to me."

Search for your mission, and fear will leave your life. Only the feeling that gives you the energy to achieve it will remain.

We are the foundation of the entire world's financial system. By obtaining bonuses, we inject them into the economies of all countries like a vaccine, gradually raising the standard of living and implementing new technologies. We won't need the management's tool of fear. Politicians will have the opportunity to serve for the well-being and prosperity of all countries because they won't be fighting for borders but instead for attracting human resources.

The more human resources exist, the more money flows into the economies of different countries. Money will not be directed towards spreading information about catastrophes and terrorist attacks in neighboring countries to intimidate us. It will be directed to specific areas prone to disasters and will prevent the possibility of losing lives without creating panic.

This calls for the invention of cures for fatal diseases or the release of existing ones that have not been put into circulation due to bureaucratic barriers. Any negative news will not be profitable. Attracting human resources will be the main concern of any state in the new reality. At the same time, all national currencies will begin to strengthen, and there will be no reason to print new banknotes for circulation.

One day I asked myself if my mission in life was to convey information about the formula or to implement the formula as a bonus system. The answer was definite—convey the information. After knowing about the formula, people will be able to implement it without me.

If you are reading this book, it means that I succeeded, and all the information about the formula has become known to people. I have already started to implement it in life and will continue to do so for all the time allotted to me in this material world. But I consider the mission already accomplished and will perceive the time of the formula implementation as a bonus, to enjoy the results.

I would like to live long enough to witness how people change their attitude toward death. We come into this world to fulfill our individual missions, and death is given to us as a reward for a job well done. I believe this shift in thinking will significantly change our perspective, and then children won't have to die. Currently, the death of children induces stress and years of suffering for those close to them. Stress and suffering teach and guide us toward fulfilling our destinies. However, if we understand that a child or any other person passes away to a new incarnation and we rejoice in that, death won't be as shocking. So, there will be no need for children to depart from life prematurely; they will have unique and meaningful purposes to fulfill in this world.

14

RELIGION AND FAITH

I had been living in Moscow for four years when I decided to send my family to America. Once, on Epiphany, friends from Sochi came to visit me. They wanted to plunge into an ice hole, but first, before the ritual they planned to stop at an Orthodox cathedral about one hundred and fifty kilometers from Moscow. I enjoy such trips, and I gladly agreed to join them. On that day, I came out of the dentist's office with a patched gum, got into the car and we set off on the journey. My gum hurt a lot, but I tried not to pay attention to the pain so as not to disrupt our plans.

When we entered the main cathedral, my friends taught me how to order a prayer for health correctly. I had to write down the names of everyone I wished good health to and give the sheet to the cashier. The woman in the headscarf carefully read the names and returned the paper, saying that these were non-Orthodox names. Then she asked, "What is your nationality?" I replied, "Armenian. And all my relatives are Armenians." She explained that I probably came to the wrong place and needed to find an Armenian church to order a prayer there instead.

I didn't want my day to be ruined, but I understood that it was useless to talk to that woman about anything. The names of my relatives were already written, and I couldn't crumple the piece of paper and throw it away. Entering the main hall, I saw an old man in black robes frozen in a prayer pose. People gathered around him, saying that elders could stay that way without eating or drinking for several days. The crowd was astonished when I approached the man and asked him to answer just one question: "Does God distinguish us by nationality?" The elder stood up and asked what I needed. I replied, "I want you to pray for the health of my relatives." He took the paper and told me to go with God. He said that he would pray for them.

My mood lifted, although my gum still hurt. We immersed ourselves in the font; the temperature was minus twenty degrees Celsius. And... a miracle happened! A real miracle that is impossible to believe in until you go through it yourself. Not only did my wound stop hurting, it healed as if a week had passed since the surgery. We recorded a video of our heroic plunge into the font and went back to Moscow with a good mood and a sense of duty fulfilled.

Long before that day, I had separated the concepts of religion and faith. The incident with the woman in the church vividly confirmed the correctness of this separation. She knew which names were in the Orthodox directory but did not comprehend that God has no directory and does not categorize people by nationality when approached with faith.

If people separated the concepts of faith and religion, our history would not have witnessed so many bloody wars based on religious disagreements. One of such bloody stories directly affected my ancestors.

All my great-grandmothers and great-grandfathers were transported across the Black Sea from the shores of the Ottoman Empire between 1905-1915 during the mass killing of Armenians. According to various estimates, during this massacre, from one and a half to two million people died. I didn't learn any of that from my relatives, although I do remember four of my great-grandmothers and two of my great-grandfathers well. The only thing one of my great-grandmothers, Oghanyan Khyngen, told me was, "When they sent us on boats, they didn't take our parents with. The water near the shore was red with blood." She managed to sail to the shores of Georgia with seven of her brothers. They never saw their parents after that. They were raised by different people but maintained a close connection with each other until old age. All the other grandmothers and grandfathers shed tears in silence. I never heard a word of hatred toward the Turks; the topic was simply avoided. They shielded children and grandchildren from their terrible memories.

This very heavy story has rooted itself in our hearts. I am sure that the descendants of Turkish warriors who killed unarmed people still carry the weight of their ancestors' actions in their souls. What were the people guilty of? There is no answer. Unfortunately, that's how the system works.

When people believe in God, they don't need a billboard to communicate with Him. Armenian churches still stand after that bloodshed, but now, instead of crosses, they have crescents. How should this be understood? Did they invite another God there?

I've been to Mongolia and visited Buddhist temples making wishes and speaking to God. In one of those temples a monk invited me to spend a night there. I slept right in the main hall; no one else was allowed in. Everyone else slept in cars or tents, but my God was with me. Faith is always with you, whether you believe in God, higher powers, or universal intelligence—choose whatever suits you; faith doesn't need advertising. Faith is one of the most important concepts to me. God and I are friends. I believe in Him, and He believes in me. Faith in oneself, in God, in one's idea, faith in the future—all these concepts are multiplied by the word faith.

I have great respect for all religious organizations preaching love, goodness, and truth. When Jesus was asked about money, he said, "Render to Caesar the things that are Caesar's."[2] Some religions revere Jesus as God, others as the son of God, and some as a prophet. In short, Jesus left a huge mark in many religions. His statement, "Render to Caesar the things that are Caesar's," [Matthew 22:21] fits perfectly with our concept. Unfortunately, he did not give an interpretation of his statement but since Caesar represented state power, it was evidently meant that state funds should belong to the state.

We do not claim state funds; we evaluate our human resources with bonuses and inject them into various financial institutions within the existing system. Bonuses can be defined as correct money or the truth serum for national currencies while for religious organizations, the bonus system is a kindred spirit.

Healing humanity from lies will lead to closer communication with higher powers. Religious organizations will undergo positive changes because only those people whose true calling is to serve God will remain there.

Everyone in the world can be rich and happy. If people are connected with the Universe, they always have positive energy. Unfortunately, there are religious figures who distort Holy Scriptures, intimidating their followers.

The new financial system will provide the opportunity to be rich in every sense, and people will flock to temples and other communities if they are treated with kindness there. Spiritual organizations will

---

2 Matthew 22 chapter — Bible — English Standard Version:
"Then the Pharisees went and plotted how to entangle him in his words. And they sent their disciples to him, along with the Herodians, saying, 'Teacher, we know that you are true and teach the way of God truthfully, and you do not care about anyone's opinion, for you are not swayed by appearances. Tell us, then, what you think. Is it lawful to pay taxes to Caesar, or not?' But Jesus, aware of their malice, said, 'Why put me to the test, you hypocrites? Show me the coin for the tax.' And they brought him a denarius. And Jesus said to them, 'Whose likeness and inscription is this?' They said, 'Caesar's.' Then he said to them, 'Therefore render to Caesar the things that are Caesar's, and to God the things that are God's.' When they heard it, they marveled. And they left him and went away."

discover new possibilities and prospects, becoming the places where answers to questions impossible to find in ordinary life are sought.

Let the Earth be a place where everyone lives a rich life in comfort and in truth. God has given us the formula for that.

Let's move on.

15

AUTHORITY AND LEADERSHIP

Authority is the manifestation of force directed towards enslaving people. It can be measured by the number of subordinates. Money, weapons, propaganda, and fear are all instruments for controlling people.

Leadership is the manifestation of personal qualities aimed at achieving results. It can be measured by the number of followers and achievements. Charisma, purposefulness, and the ability to convey information are the key qualities of a true leader.

Leadership qualities can be innate or acquired. Acquired skills develop over the years, while innate ones are demonstrated almost immediately. People can be leaders in their environment when it comes to their favorite pursuits. This is well observed in a large group setting during an event: several leaders can emerge within a couple of hours. When it comes to topics that interest people, they direct their attention towards the leaders and at some point become their associates by asking questions and participating in discussions. The leader, in turn, has an easier time capturing the attention of a larger number of people.

Since childhood, my daughter has demonstrated leadership qualities that no one has taught her. She has never ceased to amaze us, ever since I met her teacher at one of the school events. Victoria [the teacher] spent the entire evening enthusiastically telling us about our daughter. When it was necessary to calm people, Olya only needed to turn around and raise her hand—instantly, silence would fall over the class. That evening we heard many pleasant words about our child.

I remember when, around the same age, she gave me an inspiring piece of advice. It was during the beginning of my ten-year-long depression. Olya came to me with a question: "Dad, why don't you have your own money?" I asked her to clarify what she wanted to know, and she said, "So that money could be yours, and you wouldn't have to earn it." It struck me like lightning. An eight-year-old spoke the truth that I had been piecing together for eleven years by that time.

That is how things happen: when you are engaged in your own business, hints come from everywhere, and our children are conduits of the most valuable information. Up until the point that children integrate into the existing financial system, their connection with the Universe remains intact. With the implementation of the bonus system this connection will no longer be disrupted, as children will have their own money that doesn't need to be earned.

We live in a world where many leaders use authority to manage a company, a country, or a family. Don't think I won't repeat myself this time. I deliberately do this and recommend reminding yourself of these repetitions after reading the book as well. Naturally, the existing system has produced such leaders. To achieve results, they use the carrot and the stick approach, which is also applied in the old system. This is how animals are trained, but people need to be motivated, and then unique products will be born faster and more often.

Depriving someone of an annual bonus, per say, is an instrument of authority (money and fear); punishing someone for a wrongdoing through the judicial system, whether it's a child or an adult, is an instrument of authority (weapons or the use of force and fear); firing is an instrument of authority (money and fear); and competition among those in power involves the same instruments—money, fear, weapons.

In the updated financial system only leaders will be able to lead. Real leaders don't need a stick. People collaborate with them, not work for them. True leaders use their ability to convey information so that people follow them. Another tool is purposefulness—the team follows the leader towards the goal, and it is essential for the team to see this goal through the leader's eyes. The third tool is character—partners are willing to collaborate with someone who has a similar character and the same values as them. Character helps achieve results: leaders take action, then partners join in, and together they achieve the main goal. Reaching the goal is the best reward.

I often say that the existing system enslaves us, and I prove it with the examples. In this section, I want to draw your attention to the fact that not everyone succumbs to this enslavement—I know such individuals in my environment. As you've probably noticed, I don't give examples of famous people, only those from my own experience.

Before moving to America, I had close ties with my friend Vyacheslav Didenko in Moscow. At that time, he was the deputy minister, and I witnessed how he made the decision to resign from such a high position for the sake of his life principles. We had known each other for twenty years before that, and I was aware of the fact that those close to him have always teased Vyacheslav, calling him the "poor general." He has always worked not for the sake of money, but for the sake of an idea, being an example to many in power. Vyacheslav and I are constantly in touch even now, and we have a lot in common.

Another example is my father-in-law, Hamlet Tovmasyan. When he became the chief treasurer of the city, he handed over shares of his business to partners for free. The approximate value of these shares was fifteen million dollars. Now he receives a tiny pension. We help him, and he helps us. For him, too, the idea has always been above all.

I have already mentioned my grandfather, Ovanes Topchian, as a person with a kind heart. Everyone who worked under his leadership remembers him with great admiration. I recall how once I unintentionally hurt my grandmother Anya with a question: "Why do these pancakes have less meat inside than usual?" Turns out, at that time my grandparents were trying to save enough money to survive until the next pension.

There are few leaders like those people, but they exist.

I was only a tyrant in the cases when justice and money were on the scales, and people chose the money at the expense of an idea that concerned a much larger number of individuals. But now I see that as being my path to understanding the formula. Without it, I could not have realized that there is no point in fighting the system. It must be accepted as it is and understood for what it was created for. Only after that, is it necessary to find a remedy for its healing. In that case, we won't become slaves to the system; instead, the system will serve humanity and help us.

In a society where everyone is wealthy, enterprises belong to leaders-entrepreneurs who will create innovative products for people. Competition will lose its meaning.

A true leader does not use instruments of authority. There are situations when a leader with outstanding results—for example, in the space industry—may be asked about the currency exchange rate. In such a moment, hidden qualities of a person in power may surface. A leader might respond that it is not within his competence or he may express his opinion carefully, referring to competent professionals.

A person in power, however, can afford to give a clear answer, knowing that it will lead to disastrous consequences for many people. In other words, he can predict the growth of the currency and provoke millions of people to buy it when it is actually worth nothing. In this situation millions of people will lose their savings.

Unfortunately, in such cases we are often influenced by the substitution of concepts. With the introduction of the formula into the world, we will not have to mislead ourselves in pursuit of imaginary profits. There will be no point in self-deceiving or avoiding responsibility by trusting a leader in another area. We ourselves will learn to distinguish a professional's opinion from that of an amateur. After all, no one forces us to buy anything, but when we do, we are usually succumbing to the opinion of a public figure. The monetary dependence on the existing system pushes us to thoughtless actions for the sake of our own gain. This is excluded in a healthy financial system.

Let's consider the example of demanding guarantees from the government, employers, or banks... It's a concealed avoidance of responsibility. The fault lies not within yourself but with the government, bank, or employer. Yes, you're right; that's how the system is structured. And, as you've guessed, after its healing, everything will change. We will boldly take responsibility, governments and banks included. Leaders will emerge from early childhood. Freedom of choice will be inherent from the start.

At the beginning of the book, I wrote that ego drives me, and it is true. But that doesn't mean I need someone's gratitude, laurels, admiration, or let alone worship. I think any reader understands: the essence of my mission is to convey information. After completing the mission, I will accept any bonuses given to me by the Universe. These bonuses can be the happy faces of people who are rich in every sense, and there is no need for them to be grateful to me for that. Moreover, my presence in the information field will significantly decrease; I will minimize interactions on social media since I don't suffer from a cult of personality. Implementing the formula can be done without drawing special attention to myself. I am just the source of information.

Thanks to my influence, many people have already achieved significant results in different areas of their lives. That stands true, and I deliberately don't mention the names of these people. Here, you can only see some names from the reviews on our website—these people wrote about the life changes that occurred to them thanks to the formula for healing the financial system.

There was a case when one of my acquaintances, whom I could confidently classify as someone who had risen with my support, called me "a poor relative." This happened during another bankruptcy of mine. I was used to seeing this person as someone I could always turn to with any request because that's just how things were, except the opposite—I was the one helping him all the time before the bankruptcy. Even having lost everything, in his moment of need, I asked all my acquaintances to get him out of jail. He was imprisoned on suspicion of embezzlement. I could never have guessed that my tiny and insignificant favors would cause him such discomfort. I even naively assumed that all that time he was waiting for an opportunity to help me in return. But one day he didn't answer the phone when I called him and openly declared in front of all his employees, who knew me well, that his "poor relative" was calling, "probably to ask for something again."

This situation relates to the chapter about authority because in our imperfect system, many people turn into slaves and not for money, but for the power and authority that the money gives. It would be more accurate to say that money implies power over people. In my case, this rule does not work because money has always been used by me to achieve goals. I never attached any special importance to money. I often lost it and started climbing towards my goals again.

Unfortunately, in most cases people strive for money to rule over others. This should not be so, and the formula will smoothly and painlessly heal this distortion. In my book, I choose not to mention the names of people associated with any negative incidents from my life because the book is created to convey valuable information about the existence of the formula, and that is its only function.

By gaining bonuses since childhood, the next generations will not be dependent on money and will not tolerate negative authoritative power over themselves. People are the foundation of the global financial system, and each person will be aware of this. Leaders at the head of state structures will be leaders, not authority figures. And there is a big difference in that!

16

COMPETITION

In my youth, when I didn't understand the purpose of my existence, I had a passion for car racing. In a short period I crashed thirteen times and twice the car was beyond repair; it was simply sent to the scrapyard. Apparently, I still had a role to play in the material world, that is why I remained safe and sound. Looking at the mangled car, the specialists didn't believe that anyone could survive in there. I was repeatedly invited to participate in competitions, but I refused. I just loved fast driving, not competing for who is faster.

Competition is everywhere in our lives, so I decided to dedicate an entire chapter to it. The formula for healing the existing financial system incorporates the principle of complete absence of competition.

Firstly, following our formula, bonus systems should emerge in various fields of activity and people's endeavors. I will be happy to advise funds that want to develop the market for other projects to consolidate the deferred profit market.

Secondly, our system does not provide for more than ten million bonuses per day. Considering the planet's population of eight billion, it's clearly not enough. There should be other products, similar to ours, operating on the same formula.

Thirdly, a wide range of bonus systems will allow a step by step implementation of the formula aimed at healing the existing system.

Fourthly, the fund we've created will finance new products for bonus systems operating on the formula.

To create experimental prototypes and test the system, together with our partners we invested over two million dollars and we, personally, did not take a single Grand bonus. The reason is known. We obtain bonuses along with all participants in the process, and, as the first representatives of the public human resource, we know the essence of the formula: giving leads to prosperity.

Bonus Wallet is a non-commercial project; all bonuses belong to the people who earn them. Yes, it's that simple! The entire team including software developers and specialized groups (advertising, copywriting, process administration, creativity, psychology, sports, etc.) receives Grand bonuses.

We are all united by a common idea: "getting richer by giving away," and we do it with pleasure for our own benefit and for the benefit of the people. We have no desire to artificially replenish personal balances, otherwise, we would simply replicate the model of the existing financial system. Perhaps you've heard that twenty percent of people control eighty percent of all assets. These people are the biggest hostages of the existing system. If they start giving away money just like that, money will lose its value. If everything remains as it is, the system simply won't withstand the people's disagreement with rising prices and printing money with no real backing. That's where the formula comes in and works as a guarantee of reliability.

Let's return to the chapter's topic. Competition is present in all spheres of our lives. But will it be needed in a world where everyone is engaged in what they love? In our time, people are conscious enough and do not need total system control through competition.

What does competition lead to?

In sports, there is competition between rivals, clubs, and national teams—in other words, that's competition between countries. And what does it lead to?

In the economy, there is competition between employees (for the boss's chair) and between enterprises (for the local and international market). Eventually, countries compete for the right to collect taxes. What does competition between countries lead to?

In the military-industrial complex, the competition between countries is direct. Here, I won't even ask the question.

Nowadays achievements in painting, art, science, technology, and construction are not personal; these are achievements of the state you represent. They are kept in the treasury to be used in competitions between countries.

Now I will answer my own question: competitions between countries ultimately lead to a demonstration of weapons.

Unfortunately, poor presidents are unable to change anything in the realm of competition. They are forced to work for the system just to keep it afloat. The formula changes the root, the basis of competition. In the existing reality, our achievements do not belong to us, just like money. They belong to the countries, and we, the people, are simply allowed to use them. Both money and achievements must be earned by us, but will be owned by the state. Schools, universities, enterprises... They claim everything for themselves to compete with each other.

Of course, we don't mind sharing our victories with educational institutions or companies, but let's consider the fact that these achievements lead to competition between cities, regions and even countries. And this competition is dangerous. It ultimately leads to conflicts.

Can we change this system? We are already doing it. We need time and it will take more than one generation for a complete transition to a world free from competition. But for each of us individually, that time has come. People can already spend at least fifteen minutes a day on themselves, searching for their own meaning. You can do it and obtain bonuses in the meantime or just do it to change your own mindset. Our age, gender, religion, or possible disability are not obstacles here. Years and difficult life situations are given to us to fulfill our mission.

States, religious organizations, business representatives, athletes —all people, subject to the system, compete with each other. It is appropriate to recall a joke where two neighbors were given an opportunity to make two wishes. One asked the wizard to switch houses with his neighbor and immediately found himself in the other's house. Before voicing the second wish, he looked out the window and saw his neighbor enjoying the view from his former house. He realized that the neighbor was happy with the new acquisition, and his own old house seemed much better from an outside perspective. So he asked the wizard to return everything back to normal.

Many people face the same situation: we spend our lives to have more than our neighbor or colleague but don't realize our true wishes. That is another absurdity imposed by the existing financial system, and it has nothing to do with common sense.

We often compare our children with their classmates, wishing to motivate them to improve their academic performance at school. A child who wins a city math olympiad may lose at the regional level, therefore making the first achievement already seem insignificant. A talented undefeated athlete, after ending his sports career, watches as the younger generation surpasses his results. Like in the joke, people, subject to the system, live the lives of their neighbors, ignoring their own desires and, as a rule, end up never finding their true purpose.

Here it can be noted that over the past twenty-five years, I've navigated through numerous challenging life situations, each serving as a valuable lesson that propelled me towards growth and results. However, at the same time, I say that competition can get in the way of progress. Yes, indeed, even in the new system we will achieve results through difficult life experiences, given to us to delve deeper into our subject and find each of our true paths.

Let's ask any teenager who grew up in a rich and prosperous family: do they face problems? I have seen many such teenagers because I was one of them until my parents went bankrupt, just before my marriage. I can confidently state that I had countless problems in life, as well as all my acquaintances who had financial abundance.

The fact that everyone will be wealthy does not diminish the emotional factors we each possess, and we will not begin to experience less emotion. But there is a significant advantage of the formula that heals the financial system—we will have a different perception of reality. Not through the prism of artificial tools that control our consciousness, such as fear, rivalry, advertising, and competition, but through the prism of reality. In this case, people clearly understand what causes their anger or joy. They are real!

After realizing your purpose, not only do immense strength and energy appear for its realization, but also challenges arise. And in all these processes, we live our own lives full of sorrows and joys—not our neighbor's, not our classmate's, and not our colleague's.

This book won't delve into the technical details of the formula, as they can be studied in the bonus system description on our website. I only want to say that the formula has twenty levels of difficulty for earning bonuses, depending on the chosen direction. On the first level, even a baby can obtain bonuses.

The formula provides the ability to accurately assess the human resource. The resource is the foundation of the entire global financial system. Find a person who can argue with this.

What does the absence of competition bring? It gives a push to a new model of economic development. Constructive development of enterprises leads to the possibility of achieving results through joint efforts in a short period of time. There is one more aspect: a positive impact of the formula on business is brought about by new technologies (for example, artificial intelligence) aimed at creating comfortable living conditions for us.

Allow me to give you an example.

Once, Raf used a driverless taxi service in California. The autopilot is just a software that controls the car. The car doesn't need a steering wheel, pedals, and turn signals—nothing that a driver uses. There is simply one more seat for a passenger in the car. But there is a factor that slows down the implementation of such technologies very significantly. As you guessed, it's a competition.

The thing is, such a taxi can only be used in a small geographic area that has been explored thousands of times to feed the autopilot with all sorts of information about what it might encounter on the road. For example, if a hippopotamus suddenly appears, the car will simply crash into it. That is because the image of a hippopotamus was not previously uploaded into its database as a possible road hazard that requires the car to stop.

Imagine how much time, money, and human effort it would take to study and process every centimeter of all the roads and all possible situations happening on them. Just in case, I'll make a disclaimer here to avoid getting a lawsuit from the company that developed autopilot. Perhaps the situation with the hippopotamus is already in its database, and a collision will not occur. But the point here is different. The bonus system will allow such companies to implement their developments not just for a specific area in California but for the whole world.

At this transitional stage, only you and I can help businesses create comfortable conditions for the development of innovative technologies. It is necessary to develop simple and convenient programs for collecting data for artificial intelligence that absolutely everyone can use. For example, with the help of mobile apps, we can take pictures of all the roads in the world, add markings or comments to the collected photos, and earn bonuses while playing. Companies creating products based on artificial intelligence will be able to use this data for free. This way, businesses will develop new technologies at an incredibly high speed. Let's go in order.

First of all, there are thousands of such companies, and all of them are working on the same product. The one that gets there first will capture the majority of the market. The remaining companies will divide what's left, and many will have to go bankrupt. These are simply the realities of the existing system.

Second of all, these companies have to spend a huge amount of resources, both financial and intellectual, on protecting their products from their competitors, who could take advantage of the collected information.

And third of all, by joining forces, they could create this product a thousand times faster, introduce it simultaneously worldwide, earn, and receive new, even larger orders, therefore all remaining in the technological market to create new products that people need. We've already discussed how the formula affects this earlier, but practice makes perfect.

In this chapter, we have already talked about autopilots and how the formula will contribute to the development of this type of artificial intelligence. Thanks to the openness of information, brilliant software developers will be able to make a real breakthrough, and we will start noticing new assistants all around us. Robots will be introduced into all spheres of life, and this is not a scenario of the future; all these technologies already exist and are being tested in various industries.

In medicine, artificial intelligence helps diagnose illnesses and can identify special cases of diseases by comparing them with thousands of others. A doctor might take several months of research to achieve that, while artificial intelligence provides information in seconds, allowing the patient to know the correct diagnosis and start treatment faster. As a side note, similar artificial "brains" are integrated into household appliances.

In education, artificial intelligence is already taking quizzes and exams. Global changes will happen in the learning sphere: we will study at our own will, not out of the obligation to repay a debt to the failing financial system.

Artificial intelligence already exists in all industries, and we don't even notice it. For example, when typing a text, it corrects our mistakes or suggests alternative words.

However, this immense power can be destructive in the current system, as it also develops the military-industrial complex. Unmanned military equipment is actively used in interstate conflicts, and, unfortunately, we are financing this chaos.

Is artificial intelligence necessary for humanity? Yes. It is a normal step in the process of human development. However, there is a fact that no sensible reader can argue with. The existing financial system is not ready for such global changes. Despite all efforts, it cannot direct its development solely for the convenience and comfort of us, the people who are the foundation of the entire world's financial system. Due to the complete lack of financial stability and fierce competition between different countries, the time for full integration of artificial intelligence into our lives has not yet come.

The formula designed to heal the existing financial system will provide an opportunity for a technological breakthrough. By earning bonuses, every person can contribute to the replenishment of the database for artificial intelligence.

As I mentioned before, "intelligence" is a pretty fancy name for what it really is. Essentially, it refers to computer programs that compare the information loaded into them. They can even draw conclusions based on the criteria specifically entered for those conclusions.

Flying vehicles, equipped with autopilots, for everyday use are not far from becoming our reality either. It will be possible to set a route, and a vehicle will navigate an invisible overhead track on its own. This is currently used in aviation, as pilots do not steer when they see an oncoming plane, each aircraft simply has its own invisible track. And, most importantly, you won't have to issue any new laws or make innovative decisions for that to take place. Everything will change on its own along with our consciousness.

The foundation of the formula designed to heal the self-destructive financial system are we, the people who sustain it. The existing system overlooked this factor, and it has become a tremendous problem growing with each passing day. Without us, the consumers, there are no goods, services, roads, or cars—there's nothing.

The bonus created on the basis of our human resource belongs to us, as it can be earned, and its quantity is limited by time. We introduce bonuses into the existing system through our personal efforts, each contributing according to our abilities, time, and pleasure. We introduce this magic elixir, and the system begins to transform because a fundamental change is taking place. In other words, money is now printed based on the human resource which is correctly and deservingly assessed. In market conditions, all existing currencies will interact with the bonus. They will be printed less and this will strengthen their reliability.

The formula provides an opportunity to restore the system without revolutions and bloodshed, just by reinstating the missing and most crucial asset—the correctly assessed human resource. The absence of competition will enable enterprises to reach a new level of constructive implementation of new technologies, making our lives more comfortable.

17

SAFETY AND BOUNDARIES

In the previous chapters, we indirectly touched upon the topic of safety, which is relevant to each of us and can be achieved quite simply.

First, let's define the criteria for safety. What does a person need for free existence? Confidence in one's inviolability. This is the only criterion that provides complete freedom and, at the same time, limits our actions towards another person.

If you want to live in a safe world, do not exert pressure on people around you. Pressure, both mental and physical, towards other people begins with the upbringing of children. By using this very pressure, our parents prepared us to serve the system. We educate our children in the same way.

Do you remember how I explained to my son that he had to study sciences he didn't need at all? The same happens with military service preparation. Later, if necessary, our children are taken to defend the homeland and even die for it. This might have been necessary in the past but not now. Unfortunately, we don't value ourselves and don't realize that we are slaves to the existing financial system. It's not about politics, it's about us.

I was fortunate to be born as a representative of the fourth generation of orphaned children who were transported in 1905 across the Black Sea during the bloody events that were taking place in what is now Turkey. The parents were grateful to the soldiers for the opportunity to save their children, knowing that they themselves had to die in their homeland. Perhaps the past of my ancestors influenced my attitude towards children.

I remember when I was eight years old, I skipped two classes. I have to admit that I did that regularly, or rather, I attended classes from time to time, much to the delight of my teachers who missed me dearly. But that day was the only time in my mom's life when she picked up a belt, in an attempt to punish me, and tried to hurt me, but in the end, I had to sit there and calm her down for a very long time, explaining that she did not, in fact, hurt me. She cried like a child and asked for my forgiveness. In our family, children were not brought up for the system. Apparently, in 1905, the system failed significantly, and it left a mark in the genetic memory.

How to ensure safety?

Let's start by answering the question: why is our safety still relevant? In the age of technological breakthroughs, any state is capable of ensuring the safety of its citizens without involving people with weapons. The idea of weapons is not safe within itself.

In this matter, we'll have to touch on politics again—not to make accusations, but to understand what's happening. Why do nations have massive armed formations ensuring law and order within the country? It's not difficult to guess, and the very notion of "ensuring law and order" suggests that the armed people performing their duty to the homeland are a force that is subordinate to the government.

The government, in its turn, manages us with the help of armed individuals, forcing us to submit to the system. In other words, people who disagree with the existing system understand that if they don't comply, they will be punished with fines or imprisonment. We are reminded of this every day by vehicles with flashing lights and heavily armed patrol officers in bulletproof vests.

When we watch television, browse the internet, or listen to the radio, and come across reports on the latest high-profile cases and court hearings, it becomes evident that the system ensures we remain aware: we are being watched. And if we don't comply with the system, we will be quickly dealt with, without a doubt.

Of course, in the existing system, this is a necessary tool for maintaining order, but it is only needed when there are people who disagree with the system. In our time, any conscious person understands that the system is far from being perfect. We are all restrained by the daily demonstration of force, and in the end, we submit to it. But allow me to remind you that we ourselves created this system and we ourselves pay for all these attributes of power directed against us. I hope you remember that everything created by humans, including the system itself, relies on our existence.

What will happen after the gradual integration of the vaccine in the form of bonuses into the existing system? By creating our own bonuses and obtaining them through our actions, we buy goods and services. Thus, bonuses, like a vaccine, are introduced into the existing system, healing it gradually from within. Everything is simple.

Let's look a few generations ahead, but before that, allow me to tell you about the tools for personal protection. In a society where people are provided with everything they need, only one law on inviolability will work. Each individual is valuable in a healthy financial system. In the public database, the system can see how we earn bonuses. It plans income (for example, in the form of taxes) to ensure our comfortable existence.

Which personal protection tools exist today? Artificial intelligence is the first of them. It is trained in psychology and can lift one's mood. And this is just in its initial stage of training.

Besides, there are technologies that recognize a person's state based on the pulse. Pulse frequency can be determined from a distance, allowing to select people with suspicious behaviors from a crowd. By identifying a person with an elevated pulse, this technology will help prevent crimes.

These real developments, if desired, can completely replace people with weapons. For example, there could be devices equipped with cameras that would pick out suspicious people from a crowd and conduct a diagnosis right on the spot in just a few seconds. The device could look like an attractive woman or a young man, capable of conducting a test in the form of a regular conversation. If a person is emotionally unstable, the device could engage in a psychological conversation or neutralize a criminal in case of one demonstrating aggressive behaviors. It is also capable of detecting the presence of weapons from a distance. This device could be equipped with a lie detector and tools for an instantaneous arrest and neutralization of criminals.

We occasionally hear about court cases where law enforcement officers are prosecuted for exceeding the use of their power or for the unlawful use of weapons. This suggests that the human factor often comes into play, and a shot can be fired due to possible, undiagnosed mental health issues of people in uniform. Perhaps their day didn't go well, and they were in an unbalanced emotional state, but innocent people suffered because of it. Unfortunately, there are many precedents like that.

In the case of a specially designed robot that does not look intimidating, the option with emotions is excluded: the device strictly follows the instructions embedded in it to protect people. There's no need to wait several generations to start using such robots, but, alas, the system is not ready for such changes now. So what shall we do with the armed individuals in uniforms?

Here, I'll ask you to answer some questions. You will answer them to yourself—please try to be honest. Please respond with just one word: YES or NO. The answers will tell you whether it's worth reading this book further or not.

1. If you were guaranteed personal safety, would you need national borders?
2. Would you need armed individuals [military, police]?
3. Would you need places of imprisonment?

If all three answers are "No," then we have just questioned the necessity of about half a billion professions on the planet. Another couple of billion workers in the banking sector, lawyers, economists, and administrative workers are also under the same threat... This proves that the bonus should be introduced gradually. Imagine an officer in the third generation whose ancestors fought in wars, and he was raised thinking that he was meant to continue their work. For such a person, a society without borders would be a shock. But if it happens gradually, he won't ask his children to follow in his footsteps. He would support their interests and provide them with opportunities to explore other professions.

No one is to blame for the existing system. We have deeply absorbed it, and we will gradually exit it. There were times when people needed the protection of strong leaders. Unfortunately, those leaders then felt the depth of their power and started to control people. This continued for many centuries. Humanity needs time, but every person can start earning bonuses, changing themselves, and thus, the entire system right now. After all, we are its creators; it's up to us to heal it.

We need to clearly understand that radical change won't lead to the recovery of the system; it will only worsen the disease. But let's remember that the vaccine in the form of bonuses is introduced gradually; it heals the system step by step. We start earning bonuses in our free time, engaging in activities that interest us and seeking our true purpose, which people in uniforms, by the way, also want to know. This will lead to a reconstruction of consciousness and the desire to create.

Meanwhile, robots that prevent any violations of the law are gradually introduced and tested. At first, they appear in public places, then in residential areas; they can meet people at the doors of houses and wish us a good day. Their functionality may include casual conversation to lift our moods. Can you imagine how much information is available on the Internet? A robot can use it to hold a conversation on any topic. In addition, practical questions (legal, technical, and others) can be asked, and an answer will be received in seconds. You can ask it to tell you a joke too, and have a good laugh. While conversing with us on all these different topics, a robot with an attractive appearance also serves a protective function by continuously scanning those passing by and ensuring utmost safety.

All the listed technologies exist today; they are evolving at a tremendous pace. Step by step, fear, shame, and guilt will disappear from our lives. A person dreaming of living in the city of scientists, which is a thousand kilometers away from the parental home, will easily be able to travel to their dream city. After all, the world will be safe. It is our world!

18

ADDICTION

When we hear the word "addiction," our first thought is often about drug addicts. I won't dispute this fact, as I am intimately familiar with this topic through my own experiences. I deliberately distinguish these two concepts—addiction and drugs—because I am convinced: those that are addicted, change the world.

Any person we admire and wish to emulate is addicted to something. The best athletes dedicate all their free time to training in order to achieve the highest titles in the world of sports. For the greatest artists—the concept remains unchanged. They may be able to create a masterpiece leaving everyone in awe, but they are also willing to spend their entire lives creating it.

I can freely delve into discussions about addiction, as I am one of the representatives of this greatest "disease." However, this is not about me, but about the unstoppable energy and power of truly addicted individuals. Each of us has acquaintances or friends of friends whom we bring up in friendly conversations and remember them as good people. These conversations, however, usually include something similar to, "If only they quit, they would undoubtedly succeed." And that is indeed the case. Often these people overcome their destructive addictions and become examples to follow.

To fully understand the impact of the formula, life presented me with these trials as well. At the age of seventeen I became a student at the State University of Railway Communications in Rostov-on-Don. There, I gained an experience that lasted for five years. As we used to say back then, I was tightly hooked and couldn't see the light. I had considered my life worthless even before, but when I became a drug addict, I couldn't feel like a human being without two, and later, three doses of drugs a day. My life in between them just felt like an existence.

Legends circulate about the pleasure of drugs, but any addict can confirm that after a tolerance is built up, pleasure is experienced only in the absence of withdrawals and depression. When such a moment

80

arrives, any addict knows that in just a few hours they will feel terrible again and start seeking more money for the next dose. This hell continues for years, though some people experience it for their entire short lives. Unfortunately, almost none of my acquaintances from those times lived to be forty.

As always, I sought an answer to the question: what was all this for? I think this straightforward question helped me escape from the darkness. It remained unsolved for thirty years until I accepted addiction as a tremendous force, propelling me towards any set goal.

Allow me to remind you again that this book is about the formula designed to heal the global financial system, and we are examining the impact of the formula on various aspects of life. My heartfelt desire was to show people, lost in a dreadful addiction, that there is a sacred door leading them to the level of the Creator. And that time has come. But let's take it step by step.

People who are often considered outcasts of society include drug addicts, alcoholics, criminals, idlers, and anyone who doesn't meet the criteria of "normal" individuals. If we exclude medical diagnoses that require treatment in specialized institutions, what might unite all these people is a sense of protest. This feeling can arise at any age, and when it does, the lives of those individuals undergo a radical change, each in their unique way and regardless of age. I am one of them. Having gone through all the stages, I am well acquainted with the inner world of these people.

Everyone has their own hidden story, and all the stories are united by one feeling: a protest against the existing system.

Do you remember my encounter with God? I shouted at the top of my lungs, "It shouldn't be this way! What kind of God makes people suffer?" The sense of protest boiled within me, and from that moment on, I decided to do everything in my power to make the world a better place. In that instance, I was interested in the question of dependency on money; drugs were behind me, but the addiction remained. It has accompanied me throughout my life, and I am immensely grateful for it.

I don't have any intention to teach the addicts, the protesters, and the dissenters. It's pointless. Let the professionals do it. You have the formula; it will help you choose a pursuit that will become your addiction. You don't need dirty money; you will get rid of it immediately, no matter how much comes into your hands. You, like no one else, can sense lying, and the money of the existing financial system, unfortunately, is a significant lie directed towards all of humanity. The rich are deceived more than the poor for one reason— they have more money. Like all people, now you have an opportunity to choose your addiction while obtaining bonuses. Try various directions until you realize your purpose.

Here's some good news: you can search for a long time, and the bonuses will still be accumulated in the meantime. Some people might criticize me, "We work, and everything depends on us, including the idlers and alcoholics." And that's true but with a small nuance: this chapter is about all of us. Work, family, a sense of responsibility—these are all addictions expressed in various forms.

I have already stated that it's most challenging for wealthy people to reorient themselves because they depend on the existing financial system more than others. This is true but only to some extent. After reading this book, any person, including the wealthy, will understand that they're losing more by continuing to live in a false reality.

For many people, but not for all, getting money is also an addiction. Money addicts can embark on the right path by replacing a false dependency with a purpose in life, obtaining bonuses aimed at healing the existing financial system. Even presidents can feel more liberated. These individuals are in an extreme state of addiction and are enslaved by the system. No, I am not encouraging presidents to become reformers; it would simply ruin them, as it has already happened to many reformers. I understand these people and deeply sympathize with them.

When I transport passengers, working part-time as a taxi driver, I apologize for the potholes. People smile in confusion, but I am extremely aware of the fact that each of us finances the roads and everything else. That's why I apologize for the chaos we've created. But even those on the presidential needle have a path to recovery. It can be sought and revealed at any age. They can do a lot for themselves and humanity with such an immense addiction.

I listed my spheres of activity, but those are far from all the areas where I proudly served the system. I found the way to its healing after a complete understanding of all the nuances. Addiction to something is inherent in all people. It is a force, keeping us all in this world.

From the moment of birth, we depend on air to breathe, on food, on our mother, and with each passing year, dependencies, or addictions, multiply. They replace each other, transform, and represent a tremendous force and energy that keeps us focused on solving the tasks set by the Universe. In a conscious state, people decide for themselves which addiction to choose. It's even possible to make a mistake in this choice; mistakes are given to us for experience and the use of that experience later on in the future.

My experience as a drug addict gave me the knowledge to write this chapter, but could I have known about it earlier? No. Happiness lies in the fact that even if one person, thanks to this chapter, decides to switch from a destructive addiction to a pursuit for which they are willing to give all their time with joy, then another person with extraordinary creative power will appear in the world. This power will contribute to their own development and, consequently, to the development of humanity.

19

THE FORMULA AND CRIME

Let's dispel the myth of the criminal world as a world that does not obey the system. I am quite familiar with it, having been one of its representatives in my youth, when I was addicted to drugs.

As it is known, drug addicts are considered the lowest rung in this world, even notorious criminals look at them with mistrust. There is a belief that drug addicts would sell their own mothers for a dose. As everywhere, there are exceptions, like when a drug addict becomes a well-respected person of influence. But we aren't talking about me right now.

By the way, being a representative of the criminal world doesn't mean committing crimes or being incarcerated. Only a small part commits crimes and ends up behind bars.

But how do people who don't want to cause harm to others end up in the criminal world? Representatives of the law and authorities closely collaborate with criminal structures. You don't believe it? I personally was offered the position of the mayor of Sochi during my rapid career growth. No, not the way it's shown in the movies. It was an offer to finance the election campaign and even without any obligations for subsequent cooperation with me. But that's precisely how it happens: criminal authorities establish friendly ties in various governmental structures. And how could such friends refuse to help each other?

I'll share one more example from my life. Since my teenage years, I have disagreed with the system. Of course, I understood this much later, but at the time of my youth, I was seeking meaning in my seemingly worthless existence and played with death, as if deliberately provoking it to take me to the other side. Danger was my companion. It led me to the darkest alleys where I discovered the idea of being outside the law. So, even at that age, the system did not satisfy me, and I had a desire to be outside the law, or better said, outside the system. Back then, I only thought about the system in general and did not understand that injustice arises from financial inequality. As I later realized, most people who joined criminal structures were enchanted by the idea of being outside the system. But that is a naive misconception!

Legends say that according to unwritten laws, criminal authorities cannot have families, houses, or money, and that they have to give up all their possessions in favor of the idea of being outside the law. This intrigued me in my teenage years, and I eagerly began studying all the unwritten laws passed down in conversations with experienced mafia authorities.

This part of my life taught me a lot. As I understood many years later, I needed it for a complete realization of the formula that heals the financial system. This experience once again proves that there is no point in fighting against the system, whether alone or in a multimillion-member community fueled by the idea of being outside the law.

Whether you are a president, a reformer, a mafia leader, or a leader of the proletariat, you will use money from the existing system and, therefore, will submit to it. There are exceptions—people leading a reclusive lifestyle and not using money from the existing system. These include individuals with strongly expressed religious beliefs, homeless people, ascetics... Yet, even they can be subjected to the application of force by the law in case of disobedience at any moment. And here is the conclusion: it's possible to be outside the financial system but not outside the law. Even if we consider that in some countries there are untouchable people, this fact does not necessarily indicate their special status in other countries, as inviolability operates only within the framework of the legislative act of one country. Thus, within the framework of the law.

To realize this simple truth, I had to experience a lot, and my only saving grace was consistently seeking answers from God. Why do I need all this? What do I have to understand? Where is He directing me?

God guided me even when He created unbearable living conditions in my own hometown, and the representatives of the elite were afraid to be seen with me in crowded places. I was like a leper; interacting with me could lead to losing a position or a lucrative contract.

But God pushed me out of the criminal world in a different way. By then, I was already acquainted with Him, though we were not yet friends. I perceived Him as more of a parent.
I did not commit any crimes and even thought that I was a respected representative of this world. But, as it turned out, I was just bait for catching a much bigger fish, a major entrepreneur—my father.

When I was twenty-two, my father faced significant problems. He was a successful businessman, but in the 1990s, everything changed rapidly, and crime in Russia practically controlled the entire country. Up until now, my father has still not been able to recover from the blow of fate. Racketeers took everything from him and demanded a huge sum. I noticed dramatic changes in him and he seemed to have aged in just a few days. I asked him what was happening, and he told me that he was being threatened and a deadline was set for debt repayment.

At that time, I naively believed that just by being deeply educated on the criminal world, I would be able to negotiate with the crowned figure in the mafia. I knew all the unwritten laws and went to him with my father. We appeared before the "thief-in-law," as crowned authorities are called in the Russian-speaking criminal world. According to unwritten laws, you cannot argue or disagree with a thief-in-law. If you allow yourself to do it, you might face consequences: those surrounding the crowned figure could physically harm you. However, this can only happen with the approval or a specific gesture from the boss and only out of his sight.

Our conversation was short. I told the crowned figure that he was wrong. At that moment, everyone around tensed up. Only my father could stop me, and he did. It was his war, and he shielded me from the blow, taking all of the responsibility upon himself.

This situation was given to me for understanding that in the criminal world, the idea loses its importance when money is at stake. Money, as you understand, is an integral part of the existing system, and the criminals are its hostages. They are, like politicians, enslaved by the system even more than ordinary people because in their world, they create unwritten laws. In reality, criminality is part of the system, necessary for illegal money circulation. Money not accounted for in the system provides opportunities for enrichment, tax evasion, and the illegal circulation of goods and services such as weapons, drugs, and prostitution.

First of all, the formula provides transparency. Remember? You can see all the bonuses and their movement in the public repository. Second of all, the formula allows us to be healers of the system. You and I can feel it, but in a few generations that will be impossible. It will even be difficult to believe that all people, without exception, were enslaved by the financial system in the first place.

As you might have guessed, I cannot finish this chapter without telling you about the continuation of my relationship with the criminal world. But I'll talk about that a little later. Right now I would rather write about what I managed to take out of that relationship.

This chapter follows the chapters on safety and addiction

because there is a close connection between them. Most people end up in criminal structures, as they share the need of being against the system. Would you argue that there are people who are satisfied with the situation in the world, fully agree with the system and don't want to change anything?

In my rich, in every sense, life, I have not met a single person who enjoys paying taxes. Ask anyone if they would rather donate the amount they pay for taxes to a charity or spend it with a specific purpose, such as repairing a section of the road they use to get to work. The answer will indicate that even those who say that everything suits them are either lying or are deeply influenced by the system and simply do not see the obvious. Such people might not have read up to this point.

If you have all your fingers, at least on one hand, please show two fingers. I'm sure that over ninety percent of the readers showed the index and the middle fingers. Many also raised their hands with fingers pointing up. This simple test shows that we behave in the same way just because it's customary to do so—to show two fingers in that specific way. Our skeleton, by nature, is meant to function differently. The thumb is separated from the remaining four fingers, and if you relax your hand, you can see that the four fingers become slightly bent. To show two fingers, as you probably did, you have to use your thumb to hold the pinkie and the ring finger, therefore, preventing them from straightening out. It's necessary to apply effort to straighten the index finger with the middle one; otherwise, you would end up with your fingers looking like drooping ears of a bunny. It's even more challenging to raise your hand and show two fingers to an inanimate object, like a book, that can't see you. The easiest way, requiring the least resistance, is to show the thumb and the index finger in the shape of the Latin letter L.

The system has gotten so deeply into our consciousness that only the next generations will be able to act with complete awareness and a clear mind. They will be normal, conscious people, aware of the value of each action. After all, each action will be assessed with a bonus, based on the time spent doing it, and the complexity of said action.

Let's return to the story and its conclusions for which I needed all this. After our meeting, things couldn't just be left the way they were because my truth could have spread throughout the criminal world, and the throne of the crowned figure could have been passed on to someone else. There was nothing to take from my father, and he could no longer work after that incident. No one went on to talk to me; I made it clear to everyone that it was pointless. I announced that I was starting a new life, was planning to marry Kristina—we were in the midst of a relationship—and getting a job.

But it was still difficult to quit drugs. I agreed to various medical experiments, even to a procedure that induced a coma. I signed a disclaimer stating that I took responsibility for any consequences that could appear after the coma. But the attempt was also unsuccessful. This fact only further confirms my strong attachment to addictions. But the situation that followed, solved everything. To this day, I believe that it was sent to me as a key to going through yet another realization.

In the evening, Kristina and I were walking to my place. It was dark in the entrance; suddenly I felt a blow to the back of my head. A few minutes later, I found myself in the trunk of a car with my eyes blindfolded. At that moment, I didn't think about my battered, bloody head—Kristina was my only concern. For two days, while I was in the basement of some house in the woods, no one talked to me or answered my questions. They brandished their weapons and threatened to kill me. I was thinking about Kristina, as that was the reason pushing me to get out of the trap. I had to find her.

Two days later, they put me in the trunk and drove off. The car stopped, the trunk opened, and a gun was pointed at the back of my head. Then a voice said, "Count to ten." I counted. I still vividly remember the state I was in at that moment. I accepted death before it came and just counted to ten.

There was no gunshot. The voice said that they would leave me alive and that I should tell my father: debts must be repaid. I don't remember how I managed to walk through the forest to the nearest village. My whole way there, the only thoughts in my head were still about Kristina. I called home from the nearest payphone and found out that everything was all right.

My poor parents… That was another stressful situation for them! My father had a stroke some time after, and he still hasn't fully recovered: a disability, medications, and rehabilitation take up all his time.

The next day, my now deceased friend Leva and I came to the crowned person to ask a few questions about the lawlessness they had committed against me. We didn't expect acknowledgement, but the boss seemed surprised to see us and spoke to us in the most friendly manner. He said, "Do you really think that I'm involved? Such matters are punished in our world…" We knew that without his stories. After the meeting, I put an end to it all and started a new life.

As always, I gained many benefits from this story. Everything is given to us for learning and achieving our true purposes. While I was in the basement, I didn't even have a hint of withdrawal symptoms. That helped me understand that they were always just in my head. This can be confirmed by any addict who ended up in prison and suddenly discovered that there was no withdrawal. God not only pushed me out of the criminal world but also freed me from drugs. I also learned a lesson that brought me closer to unraveling the formula for healing the existing financial system. My dear reader, you already know what happened next.

When we start using the formula, there will be no crime for one simple reason: the system will be healthy, and there will be no sense in the idea of being outside the law.

New generations, including you and me, will create the foundation for a healthy system designed to serve humanity. The ranks of the criminal world will thin out, and soon only people with mental deviations would willingly want to remain there.

A normal person cannot consciously harm others. Plus, by that time, we will have friendly robots with artificial intelligence helping people in a healthy society.

20

LOVE AND FAMILY RELATIONSHIPS

Love is the greatest of words that all religious scriptures are filled with. Love is a feeling that each of us strives to achieve throughout our lives. From the first sentences of this chapter, I want to declare: YES! The formula is directly connected with love. As we have already seen, it opens the way not only to financial independence but also to understanding the world and ourselves, to a conscious perception of reality, and, of course, to love.

Let's start with family relationships. Family is a cell of society; and society, as we understand it, is the fundamental basis of the entire world's financial system. But have you seen many families bonded by true love?

If so, let's imagine this situation. I apologize for the frankness ahead of time, and if you are a religious person or are under eighteen, you can skip this chapter. For those who decided to read further, here we go.

Imagine this: one of the people in a relationship caught the other one in an explicit sex scene, unlike anything they had experienced before. What, in your opinion, will happen to love at that moment? I think that more than ninety percent of the readers are judging me right now, thinking that such a thing, or anything similar to it, could never happen to them. Then another question arises: what is love? Isn't it a feeling of absolute satisfaction for the positive emotions experienced by our beloved partner? Then why don't we feel these emotions when witnessing an explicit scene involving our loved one with someone else? Where is our joy? Why don't we join to enhance the pleasure? Where has love gone?

I apologize again for such intimate details, but they provide understanding: what we call love, is not love at all. Words like possession, agreement, obligations, and friendship are much more suitable here. Each couple can use a different word to describe their relationship.

Let's recall history; without it, our consciousness would be incomplete. The fear of death for adultery is embedded in our consciousness. Our ancestors stoned people without trial and examination. Even an innocent person could be shamed and killed in front of the whole community. Nearly everyone participated in this violence, driven by the fear of retribution.

All these intense emotions could not disappear without a trace. Talking with children about sex is still a forbidden topic in many families. By the way, my daughter Olya and I discuss her thoughts on this topic more openly than she can with Kristina.

Since the time when physical strength played an important role in society and weak women literally belonged to their husbands, many years have passed. But still, echoes of a sense of ownership remain in many families.

The formula is not a panacea for all troubles, but finances play an important role in our reality. Nowadays, physical strength has been replaced by financial strength, and we often exert pressure on our "loved ones" through the prism of finances.

The formula is not designed to directly teach us how to love. That being said, by influencing the existing financial system, it will help distinguish the concepts of love, family, friendship, and partnership. Financially free people will be together by mutual desire.

Speaking from my own experience, over the twenty-seven years of my life with Kristina, whether together or apart, we have gone through all the possible stages of relationships. In the first two years, she left me for her parents several times. That was a challenging period: we were trying to get used to each other's personalities, and Raf helped us find compromises. For the next eight years after that, my business absorbed all of my time. Meanwhile Kristina made our house a home and was raising both Raf and Olya while getting them involved in various activities and sports. They were winners of many major violin competitions. Unfortunately, I missed all of that; my role was to ensure prosperity and proudly attend all of our children's award ceremonies.

Then came the period of bankruptcy, persecution, and depression, which gave me the opportunity to spend more time with the children. I am grateful for that period of my life. Kristina went to work and replaced me, providing the family with everything we needed.

But financial obligations after bankruptcy grew like a snowball. I had to fulfill them, ensuring both the family's safety and proper conditions for the children's development. The decision was made to send the family to America. Kristina couldn't work there, if we don't count domestic responsibilities and the process of adaptation in a foreign country as work.

The children went to school, and I became a festive dad again. I visited my family twelve times in four years and, naturally, financially provided everything for them. During those four years, I managed to fulfill all financial obligations in Russia and reunite with my family. Now I am fully engaged in my life's work and derive true pleasure from it, while Kristina has been working and helping me move forward for the past six years.

We went through the stages of passion, friendship, agreements, hopelessness, and new agreements. Now, looking back on everything, I can say: she is my person and I am hers. I love her so much that if she wanted a hot guy with a six-pack, I would gladly provide her with that opportunity. She deserves everything she wants because she is the love of my life.

When the formula helps heal the financial system, everything will be different. We won't have to substitute concepts that define our essence. The meaning of measuring strength with money will disappear, as everyone will have it. Money will be just a tool for settlements, and each family member will become self-sufficient and independent in choosing their desires. Love will be real. Friendship, partnership, sex—all these concepts are absolutely different and can coexist in one family.

21

SEX

I touched upon the topic of sex in the chapter about love, but this subject requires special attention. There's no need to argue that powerful leaders have influenced us through sexual relationships since ancient times. It was necessary for us back then; otherwise, we wouldn't have created such a financial system. Or rather, just a system.

Everything in life happens to us for some given reason. There are even references about sex in the Old Testament. People chaotically satisfied their animal instincts; both men and women engaged in relations with each other, the weak were simply raped. People got infected with diseases and died in massive numbers. This had to be stopped.

Strong leaders enacted laws prohibiting indiscriminate relationships. They punished disobedience with shame and even death. Yes, perhaps that was necessary in the ancient world, but we don't live there. People could be punished for lustful thoughts about sex. If a husband was jealous, he could bring his wife to the leader without any evidence of infidelity, and the judges of that time would be in charge of deciding her fate. Now we live in a civilized world, but what has changed?

Let's first separate this concept into sex for the continuation of life and sex for pleasure.

For the continuation of the species, we engage in sex, on average, from one to four times in a lifetime, judging by birth rates. Different countries have various birth rates. This is the influence of politics and other external factors. Somewhere, families are paid allowances to motivate childbirth, while in other countries penalties are imposed for having too many children. That is what a sick financial system has led us to!

Kristina and I can confidently call ourselves an exception: we decided never to use any means of contraception; abortions are out of the question either. In other words, we combined sex for pleasure with sex for procreation. In twenty-seven years of life together, we have been blessed with two wonderful children. And if the world gives us more, we will be even happier.

In the matter of sex for procreation, the formula will provide new opportunities, and people will have motivation to give birth. It's no secret that many families plan the number of children they will have, based on their financial capabilities. I have already written that over time, we will get to bracelets that infants will wear, obtaining bonuses for their pulse, movement, and, as they grow, for crawling, walking, and so on.

The time has come. Technology allows us to create such bracelets easily. Our Grand Time fund will finance their production as soon as we receive applications from entrepreneurs willing to manufacture these bracelets. Naturally, after a thorough analysis of all proposals, we will finance the best option. This will provide even more motivation for the continuation of the species. Children will be able to gain bonuses from birth and practically secure their own future, even if it only happens in several generations.

A person is self-sufficient in every sense. The current financial system does not take this fact into account, but the formula will provide this opportunity.

Here, you can accuse me of imperfections in the formula. I understand that in this scenario, I myself would gladly give the opportunity to bear children from me to thousands of women. The conditions would be mothers' health, a common last name, and a healthy financial system that ensures safety and creates conditions for the up-bringing of children. This way, you and I will quickly increase the world's population. But this is unrealistic. Do you need any arguments?

Women decide for themselves how many children to have and who will be their fathers. In a prosperous life, many factors will influence this decision. Freedom, self-realization, responsibility... These are restraining arguments for women. We have long crossed the threshold of awareness, and the formula will only enhance it. We are reasonable people.

Sex for pleasure

I understand that this book may be read by religious figures, officials, judges, strict parents, and other people with beliefs in the existence of rules in sexual education.

If you are one of the people listed above, for example, a high-ranking official and even your own children see you in a suit, please answer one question: did you poop today? What? Does the question embarrass you? Is the question unethical, in your opinion? Or is it none of my business when you poop?

Then please answer another question: is it any of your business how, with whom, and in what positions I derive pleasure from sex? If after my questions you still believe that you have the moral right to regulate people's sexual relationships, then next time, while sitting on the toilet, take a computer instead of a newspaper and start looking for your true purpose, whether you gain bonuses or not.

Sexual satisfaction is one of the most emotionally colorful physical sensations, given to us by nature. We have no moral or normative right to forbid people to derive pleasure from sex in any of its manifestations. The only criterion applicable in this aspect is safety. That is, people should engage in sex by mutual consent.

All rules of sexual education are created to control people through fear. Everyone peeks into our underwear whenever they want. First, our parents teach us moral behavior; then they pass the baton to the entire outdated system, from religious denominations to state figures. By the way, even in the criminal world, there are so-called moral rules for control .

In this sense, I am a representative of traditional orientation— not by conviction, but by my own choice. If your physical body wants to scratch behind your ear, no norms are required for that. But if that is an intimate place of your body, you are obliged to follow the rules, right? A massage brings the same physical satisfaction as sex, but a masseuse adheres to the client's safety. Pleasure and healing properties from sex are greater than those from a massage, only one cannot control us through the prohibition of massages—we won't die without them, while without sex, we simply wouldn't have been born.

All sorts of manifestations of sexual minorities—parades and protests—are caused precisely by these prohibitions. I am sure that not everyone but many people with non-traditional orientations came to realize their identity due to their subconscious disagreement with the existing system.

Disagreement with the system could arise in various forms because of different reasons: from parents' interrogations and visits to the gynecologist to cases of harassment, where a teenager is afraid to talk about it to avoid condemnation.

In the first case, the representative of the system is the parent who breaks the child's individuality and leads them to the doctor. In the second—it is a judging society.

Allow me to say it one more time: if people have an itch behind the ear, they don't fight for the right to scratch it. If one of a person's dozens of erogenous zones happens to be in the mouth or anus—what has changed? It's their mouth, just like their ear. It's their anus! And what connection do we have towards their personal physical expressions?

You can put plastic straws and cigarettes in your mouth, even your own fingers but why is another organ off-limits? What distinguishes a female mouth or anus from a male's? From a safety standpoint, cigarettes and plastic straws cause more harm. What does society have to do with an individual's personal preferences? Teenagers decide that society is against them and express disagreement with the system.

As you can see, this disagreement manifests itself in various spheres of our reality. Some people consciously violate traffic rules, which is also a disagreement with the system; others throw trash outside the bin, showing their protest; someone doesn't pay taxes or turns to a life of crime; there are those who change their sexual orientation, hate their parents, and some hide within themselves and stop communicating with the world.

All these things are manifestations of disagreement with the system that the formula is designed to heal through the gradual introduction of bonuses that belong to us, humans. In a healthy system, every person is valued, and each of us chooses the society in which we feel comfortable.

This chapter is not meant to criticize the existing system and certainly not to find those to blame. You and I are both officials and religious figures. We created the system ourselves, and we will be able to heal it when we understand the causes of the disease. For this purpose, we systematically study all important aspects of life and the influence of the formula on them.

The main advantage of healing the system with the help of the formula is that the system starts to change together with us. By gaining bonuses, by searching for our purpose, we dedicate time to ourselves which leads to the reassessment in consciousness—we begin to value ourselves. Simultaneously, we introduce the missing ingredient into the system in the form of an appreciated human resource.

The formula starts working from the moment we begin to look at the world through a different perspective. Not through the prism of the old system, but openly, discerning all the colors and shades of our own space.

Let's move on!

22

BUSINESS EXPERIENCE AND THE INFLUENCE OF THE FORMULA

As I mentioned before, I had many business projects, both successful and unsuccessful. But, unlike my ancestors, I was fortunate to be free from the influence of the monetary system.

In the history of my parents' families, there is a legend about a long war for the mints[3]. I accidentally learned about it from my namesake in a casual conversation. By the way, my real last name is Zeitunian. I took the pseudonym Grandi relatively recently.

During the conversation, after hearing my mother's last name — Topchian—my namesake literally felt sick. He asked me again, thinking that I knew the story and was just joking. When he realized that I was telling the truth, he told me that somewhere about four generations before us, the Topchian family had their own mint. They minted gold coins and were a very wealthy dynasty. As I understood, the Zeitunian family also had some connection to this gold, which led to a feud between the two dynasties.

Unfortunately, I don't have many details on the story. When I asked my mother, she said that she found out about it on the day of her engagement from Grandma Baytzar. Grandma cried a lot, but she gave her blessing to my parents' matrimonial alliance. My mother couldn't get any more information since both of the grandfathers reacted very painfully to any questions. Apparently, the wounds were still fresh.

I perceived this news of past hostility as another sign leading me to the formula. As the firstborn, I became the fruit of reconciliation between two feuding dynasties. Who, if not me, should make changes to the outdated system causing bloodshed?

I was lucky—I always looked at the world with my own eyes, not through the prism of the system. I remember when I was eight years

---

[3] places where coins were being manufactured.

old, I traded my stamp collection for beautiful bottle caps, which angered my mother. She thought I had been deceived and couldn't understand that the caps were more important to me. I didn't care about their value; I considered it a profitable deal.

Since then, not much has changed. To achieve results, I sold all my property and left my parents to live in a rented apartment while I also remained without my own housing. I'm very ashamed that every month my creditors send me receipts for my debts, but all of this is trivial if compared to the results I see every day. Of course, my relatives occasionally reproach me for that, but I am immensely grateful to them for their understanding and support. We are moving towards our set goal and see results every day. When the goal is beyond one human life, every step that brings us closer to it is already a result.

It has always been important for me to do business for the benefit of people. I treated money as a tool for calculation and, as you understand, often lost it.

The existing sick system creates harsh conditions for business. Competition, absorption, dumping—all these are tools of the old system that closes the eyes of many entrepreneurs and pushes them to cut employees' salaries, increase working hours, worsen the quality of products and so on.

Such business leaves no room for creation and forces one to choose between bankruptcy or transitioning to a format of competitive advantage at the expense of quality, salaries, and constant deception.

As you might have guessed, I preferred bankruptcy. I went on, emerging from multimillion-dollar debts to build a new business. Now I am very glad that I had to overcome such challenges many times. With each new bankruptcy, I gained a vast wealth of practical knowledge, getting closer and closer to the formula for healing the global financial system. But how I grieved and engaged in self-deprecation in every case of bankruptcy! Joy came much later with an understanding of why I needed all this.

You and I can imagine what business will be like after the system is healed. The bonus infusion will sort us out, and those who are motivated not by the money of the old system but by their desire to be useful will remain in their positions. Everyone will recall their purpose and, being free from slavery, will be charged with energy.

From personal experience, I can say this energy is incomparable to any powerful drug; it's an indescribable state of happiness for a lifetime. The awareness of purpose alone provides unforgettable emotions and the necessary tools in the form of knowledge and experience to achieve success in any activity.

Let me share a practical example. My company, SochiGrandStroy, which I mentioned earlier, was assigned the responsibility by the administration to manage a unified billing center that handled monthly utility payments. The center had one hundred and seven staff members, and I once again faced a choice: either raise the cost of utility payments or fix the clearly inflated structure of the unified billing center. Naturally, I made a decision in favor of ordinary people, shocking advisers who suggested raising utility tariffs. As a result, only four of one hundred and seven people remained part of the staff, and there is no mistake here; the number is absolutely accurate: exactly four people, passionately engaged in their work.

I'm not trying to convince the reader of my humanism. Not at all. When I face a choice, I can easily make a decision and fire people. If you dig into the past, you can find individuals who caught heat from me, quite literally. But they knew why, and I have no regrets. People who have to deal with me fall into two categories: the first hates me to death, while the second loves me wholeheartedly. I haven't learned to evoke neutral emotions.

This example illustrates that a person who has found passion can achieve more than any educated specialist deceived by the old system.

In the new system, there won't be any need to face such choices and fire employees. Consequently, in similar companies, four people will work efficiently, while the other one hundred and three will also show themselves but in their true callings. Wealthy individuals won't sit idly, creating the illusion of work.

Here's some more good news: there is no age limit or wasted time when it comes to reevaluation and transitioning to another field of activity. Participants of our experiments genuinely live new lives full of positive emotions, meaning, and immense energy driving them forward, thanks to the formula for healing the financial system.

Olga Frolova from Moscow writes in her review that after understanding the formula, huge changes occurred in her life. She always thought that due to her profession, she would always be helping celebrities and be satisfied with others' results, forever remaining in the shadow of their glory. Now she sings on stage herself, being a rising star in the entertainment industry. This is just a small part of the changes happening in our community, and we observe them every day.

Realization comes quickly to people with little wealth since we are less susceptible to the influence of the system—there's nothing to lose. People with more wealth, due to an old habit imposed by the system, want to buy more bonuses, therefore slowing down their process of understanding the formula. Nonetheless, it also yields results.

You and I have just discussed another aspect of the formula, and we see that it will radically affect improvements of the business industry. This aspect helps us find our true purpose. People heavily influenced by the existing system will need more time to transition to the new financial system, but there are exceptions.

In our time, practically all enterprises are established to generate profit, and quality is improved through competitive struggle. With this approach, the method of the old system comes into play, extracting that profit from us, consumers, who pay money.

If we look two generations ahead, businesses will be exclusively run by those people who have true vocation for that. There are many such individuals even now, and I consider myself one of them. When starting any business, an entrepreneur is focused on creating products and improving their quality; profit is a bonus but not the result of that process.

The future is already here, but not everyone has realized it yet. For the age of the planet, two generations are a short period. The future will come for each of us when we are ready to accept it.

23

HOW THE IDEA TO CREATE THE GRAND TIME FUND EMERGED

After countless attempts to find investors in different funds, we decided to create a fund and become the investors ourselves.

A bit of background...

By the twist of fate I found myself in America. Staying in Russia was unsafe for my family. The so-called Silicon Valley turned out to be another valuable experience for me. Raf and I quickly adapted. Raf even decided to settle there and moved from Chicago permanently.

The funds of Silicon Valley, centered around Stanford University, can be considered the managing company of the entire global economy. Indeed, Google, Facebook, Apple, Tesla, and several other enterprises in this tiny village, were created by those funds. Each of these enterprises has an annual turnover that can be compared to the turnover of many countries. The funds themselves manage trillions of dollars.

But what attracted us was the energy of hospitality; we felt at home among like-minded people. Every day, events were held where talented entrepreneurs from various fields communicated with each other and presented their projects, hoping to stand alongside Google and Uber.

In short, we were among our own, but no one understood us. No one from the financial sphere, of course, as they have something to lose. They are controlled by the fear of change, which prevails over reason. In the Valley, I understood the psychology of investors well. It was there that the idea was born to create our Grand Time fund and act as the formula teaches.

The idea to create the Grand Time started its journey when the founders' accounts had a negative balance of 2.5 million dollars, and all this money was invested in a "non-profitable project," according to skeptics and adherents of the old financial system.

Here, I want to make a clarification. I constantly criticize the old system, and you might get the impression that Don Quixote decided to fight the windmills. That is not the case at all. I will do everything in my power to prevent the old system from collapsing. The essence of the new system is to heal the old one.

It is for this purpose that we eagerly tried to explain the benefits of our project to the investors. You just need to get a vaccination, and the disease will disappear. In other words, it is necessary to introduce bonuses into all areas of human activity from birth to death.

That's an easy way to protect ourselves from a deadly disease. Still, a skeptical reader might ask how much time and money it will take. One human lifetime won't be enough for all people on the planet to become wealthy. But the vaccine itself starts working instantly. As it is introduced in various directions, the system recovers.

Our invested 2.5 million is a drop in the ocean. I will effortlessly invest 2.5 billion dollars, even if I have to take them as a loan, since these investments would not be put into a business, but into a new market of deferred profit. This market will enable the turnover of trillions of dollars, simultaneously healing the existing system.

I can notify both skeptics and readers who have understood everything long before—the time has come! Many people with a strong conviction to be on the team are joining our community. To my question why they do it, each of them replies, "I feel with my heart— this is mine." Mysticism? No, it's just that the time has really come.

Here is Laura's feedback coming from Armenia: "I went through a period of time where I lost myself. It happened due to a forced move during the interethnic conflict in my country. Suddenly, I realized that, because of my nationality, there was no place for me in the country where I had lived my entire conscious life. In an instant, I lost my home, friends, job, and all my familiar places. I moved to my "historical" homeland of Armenia and entered the monastery of Geghard. In my prayers at the monastery, I had one wish that I expressed to the Lord: to find new possibilities open up in my life. And it happened. I was gifted a Grand bonus! It was a mystery to me at first, I didn't even know what it was, but I understood clearly—this is my new opportunity. I found myself at the origins of a project aimed at healing the system that took everything from me. I learned to love the world again and gained tremendous energy for life. Now I am launching the Grand Time investment fund in Armenia where I will be a representative of this grand project. In my prayers, I thank the Lord for this gift."

Under no circumstances should any events be rushed. I have already mentioned that if the whole world transitions to a new financial system in one day, nothing will work. The collapse will happen immediately. It's like a dose of a vaccine given to one patient instead of curing a thousand people. That patient would simply overdose and die.

By the way, such an incident has happened in my life. I was facing the path to the next dimension, but doctors pulled me back, as usual, because it was not my time to go—I still had things to finish in this world.

So, the second objection from skeptics can be answered by anyone in our community of thousands. We are already earning bonuses and developing the new financial system. We can buy certain goods and services with our bonuses. The joy of acquiring items with bonuses far exceeds the satisfaction of buying something with a regular salary. After all, we obtain bonuses through enjoyable activities, and we don't treat them as money earned through hard work.

It is not in our interest to exchange them for money because money is subject to inflation. We create demand for our bonuses by integrating them into new products, such as stores where you can make purchases with bonuses or payment systems where you can pay with bonuses without converting them into money. We create services that can provide additional income from bonuses, such as deposit storage or investment in businesses that follow the formula.

Community members have already bought coffee machines, power tools, bags, watches, handmade products; they paid for advertising in the community and enrolled in online courses using bonuses.

Our genetic code, passed down from generation to generation, dictates to most of us that money doesn't come easily. Engaging in a favorite activity, receiving bonuses for it, and buying goods with them might seem like something out of the realm of fantasy to many. But the truth is that money should serve people and be a regular tool for measuring the time and efforts of each person. Everyone should receive money for actions that benefit society and themselves as part of that society.

In the existing reality, it is not easy to realize that money can be paid for pleasure. However, these examples, among other concepts discussed in the book, prove the reality of a new era. We have given value to everything except ourselves.

If anyone thinks, after reading this book, that the bonus system is developing actively, that's not the case. We are still at the initial stage. Our Grand Time fund has invested in three projects; they are in the stages of development and testing. We haven't started attracting money yet. We'll start doing that after the book is released, so that there's no need to explain obvious things to investors. I would be happy to advise other funds looking to develop the deferred income market.

Raf and I have decided to recruit Stanford students to work for the fund, solely based on ideological considerations. First of all, people making investment decisions should not be tempted by the money of the existing system. Second of all, these individuals should have a strong desire to personally contribute to the healing of the financial system. This university conducts student selection based on similar principles. Moreover, for the most part, these students have never needed money and have not been dependent on it. We will distribute the book among them and conduct a thorough selection. Then we will invite the best people to work for highly paid positions in the fund. While working, they will be able to obtain bonuses like all users of bonus wallets, no more and no less. We also need general partners committed to the idea. There are such people in the major league of venture investors. We intend to assemble a team of leaders in finance, public trust, legal and computer industries, artificial intelligence, blockchain development, and other professions. It is important to create a team that wants to make the world a better place, with the finest leader in charge, not me. I will advise teams of all funds wishing to take part in the development of the human resource assessment market. This will require a lot of time for traveling. I will give the dividends from my role as the general partner of the Silicon Valley fund to Raf. He has already taken responsibility for the financial well-being of our family, so it'll be convenient for each of us.

At the moment, we are investing with loaned money. We are launching new funds with a team formed from the most dedicated individuals who joined us from different countries: software developers, managers—basically, everyone who can evaluate prospective formula projects appropriately. I know that we will face many challenges that will each teach us a lesson; there will also be many successes that will inspire us. Everything will happen the same way it does in the life of any full-fledged person.

A trip without stops is not a journey. You can miss out on everything interesting.

24

ADVERTISING

Advertising is a companion and a comrade of a fading financial system—in any situation, it always remains profitable. Only profit can turn out to be waste paper, and those working in the media are well aware of this. Not everyone, but those who directly have to carry out the orders of the authorities. They, like us, are all interested in the stability of the system. And just like politicians, they are hostages of the fading financial system.

When choosing a path to making good profit, any person will prefer the right and most ethical one. It doesn't matter what to advertise: chips or the power of the state. The only important aspect is knowing that your advertising is beneficial.

If we're talking about chips, then, for the same money, any person would rather advertise the healthier brands of chips. If we're talking about the power of the state, then the choice between advertising weapons or the well-being of the population will also be an easy one to make.

Healing the financial system will lead us to advertising the state with a happy population and open borders to attract citizens from other countries. People are the foundation of the entire world's financial system.

If you look into the archives of mass media of the city of Sochi from 2004 to 2009, you will understand how well I am acquainted with this "temptress" named Advertising.

Every day on the news channels, they would broadcast about the lawlessness in the city's municipal services. I was called "the culprit of this lawlessness," who "transferred the entire residential fund to a private company and created chaos."

The attacks intensified, especially during the elections for the next mayor of the city. Five mayors were replaced within five years. And all those years, as I mentioned above, my company managed to keep housing maintenance rates unchanged while the prices for goods and services kept rising.

As always, my choice was in favor of common sense. Despite the negative information that pursued me from all different directions, I did not spend any funds on refuting accusations through counter-advertising campaigns. It was more important for me to do my job well and, at the same time, not raise rates for the general population.

Advertising is not always obvious and labeled. There is a hidden form of it too, which affects public opinions and their choice of goods and services. Such type of advertising can occur while we are watching movies, for example. We involuntarily notice what our favorite characters are wearing, what cars they drive, or what water they drink—in general, everything we see in movies is transferred to stores and is in demand.

Advertising has existed since ancient times. Our ancestors used similar spears while hunting mammoths, but over time those spears were improved. This indicates that people saw whose spear worked better in the hunt and made the exact same one for themselves.

This type of advertising exists even today and works better than all others. It's called word of mouth—people pass information from mouth to mouth. It is the strongest and most effective; political technologists fear it because all tricks are either temporary or pointless when fighting the truth.

The good news is that advertising will always exist. It is necessary in all spheres of life for providing information about new products and services available to us.

I do not recommend separating the concepts of advertising and information. This separation simply should not exist for us because it is a product of the old system, which the formula is meant to heal.

The said separation creates a division into "expensive" and "very expensive." If we see, let's say, a new vacuum cleaner model being advertised on social media, we can be sure that the advertiser paid a fairly high price for that ad. We realize that it's just another ad and scroll past it. However, if we see the same vacuum cleaner in a post of a favorite blogger we trust, then the fact that he is showing it to us as an advertisement, which costs more, may make us want to buy it. But the blogger is not an expert on vacuum cleaners; he could be any one of us. Now, if we see that same vacuum cleaner presented by an expert blogger, someone who is known to give expert ratings for various household appliances, then the cost of that ad would be even higher because it creates a higher trust level and is presented to us most often as just plain information.

Of course, there are many other factors: for example, where the advertisement is posted and how wide of an audience it has an ability of reaching. It may appear in movies or specialized shows and is also perceived as just "information." But in the end, the buyer pays for all of that. The buyer being you and I.

Let's define the drawbacks for the vacuum cleaner manufacturers. They have to spend a fortune before starting to make a profit. Besides, there are risks that competitors may go through the same advertising channels with a higher quality vacuum cleaner and a lower cost.

But advantages also exist: if everything works out, the manufacturer will make a profit (minus advertising expenses).

For us, the drawbacks consist of additional advertising costs. We may not be aware of a better-quality vacuum cleaner that costs half as much as the first one simply because it is not shown to us in said advertising due to the manufacturer's lack of that added value.

This calculation can be applied to any product to understand that in the existing system, advertising is set up for maximum return on the money the system gave us, evaluating only our labor.

No one is specifically to blame for this. We had to go through this path of evolutionary development in conditions of competition: battles for shelf space and working places; enmity between nations and religions. All of this is accompanied by propaganda in the media.

I don't distinguish between the concepts of advertising and propaganda because this separation of concepts is also the product of the existing system. We are urged to buy a vacuum cleaner and urged to fight against an "enemy" nation practically by the same methods.

Changes will undoubtedly occur in the vast information industry because only those people who truly want to work there will, for the sake of fulfilling their mission and becoming true versions of themselves. These people will have a real desire to only declare the truth about products, services, and everything happening in the world. There is also a sense of our own responsibility.

Do you remember the time when I drove people and apologized for the potholes in the roads? This precisely relates to understanding our responsibility for everything that happens because at the end of the day, we are the ones who pay for everything, roads included.

In the information sphere, as well as in other areas of life, the formula opens up more possibilities. By viewing ads, we earn bonuses. Do you remember the example I mentioned about gaming platforms?

Any social media platform that works based on the formula will show us ads for which we accordingly will earn bonuses since all of our actions on that platform, including viewing ads, are worth something. Our first advantage is deferred profit. Social media cannot exist without people. This realization opens up to us as soon as we start to value ourselves. When does that happen? It happens during the bonus acquisition for ad views.

We will clearly begin to realize the importance of our presence on social media. Knowing that, we will change our approach to likes, comments, posts, ratings on ads, and accounts in general. We will take our actions more thoughtfully since we will understand that the promotion of that ad, post, or account depends on our actions.

We will be giving our honest opinions, and such advertising will work like those primitive spears did, back in the ancient world. Like the vacuum cleaner, bought by our friend who now expresses enthusiasm in view of its functionality. Word of mouth.

With the introduction of the formula, our mentality changes: we hear and speak the truth more. Social media won't have an opportunity to inflate views because bonuses are awarded for that, and the formula strictly controls the process. Anyone can see bonuses in the public repository, and that is another huge plus.

Remember, I mentioned that I don't differentiate between the concepts of "information" and "advertising"? Let's consider that and take a look at this book as an example. The book provides information about the formula aimed at healing the existing financial system. In other words, it advertises the formula. Additionally, the book contains information about the Grand Time fund, the Bonus Wallet, and me, urging every reader to find meaning in life by engaging in their favorite activities. Hidden advertising is also present here. For instance, a talented programmer, lawyer or a professional from related fields cannot remain indifferent after reading this book. I will be glad to look at the applications on our website, though now this advertising is not so hidden. All the above listed information can be considered and called "advertising", especially if I paid a renowned author to write about it. Countless more examples can still be described, but I prefer taking actions and encourage the reader to do the same.

If you enjoy doing something and have found your path, don't wait for the bonus system to appear specifically in that industry. Start doing it even without bonuses, develop your skills for fifteen minutes a day, and you will see changes in your life.

Even without bonuses, you will begin to value yourself by dedicating time to your dream.

25

FORMULA AND TRUST

I don't think that after reading this chapter, everyone will be ready to fully accept the formula, and that's absolutely normal. I strongly recommend rereading the book from time to time to refresh the information received.

The reality in which we have to live affects our consciousness, and we can get caught up in the daily race with our neighbors and colleagues.

But even after reading this book once, each of us is one step closer to a rich life of a creator, gained through awareness. This book is a treasure that can be shared. Like the formula, the book carries the "giving away and getting richer" effect.

If we were to present the formula for the healing of the global financial system as a mathematical one, it would look like this: public human resource equals public capital. As you understand, this equality is being severely violated because the current system has not properly valued the human resource. Based on the data from various sources, the average value of the public capital is estimated at one quadrillion dollars. This means that with the condition of a single bonus evaluating the human resource, the potential growth in the value of one Grand could reach approximately forty-three thousand dollars. Naturally, there are accompanying factors; for example, other non-profit organizations operating according to the formula will emerge, and our bonus will share its value with their bonuses evaluating the human resource. Additionally, public capital grows annually, which positively affects the growth in the value of the human resource. Another factor is trust, which can raise the value much higher than forty-three thousand dollars per Grand. Although as its parents, we can significantly overestimate the value, as is known, market valuation depends on demand, and demand is created by people obtaining their own bonuses. In order for us to adequately assess our assets, the formula includes graphs showing the cost of extraction, and other bonus projects operating according to the formula will appear on the fund's website. Growth should be slow and steady.

The use of the formula predisposes to trust among people.

Trust can be expressed in two ways. The first is when you can give a person you barely know the keys to your apartment where all your savings are kept, with the key to the safe hanging in the bunch, of course. This is absolute trust. Such trustful people often hear the words: "Fate will test you when you get fooled once. It'll be a good lesson for the rest of your life," or something along those lines.

Indeed, the moment when you'll be able to trust everyone at all times has not yet come. But the number of those who have real trust for everyone deep in their hearts keeps growing, meaning that those times are not too far ahead.

The second option is redirected trust. It means that there are intermediaries between us and the person to whom we give the keys to our apartment. These may be surveillance cameras, alarm systems, security, biometrics, etc.

In this case, we trust a stranger and all the listed intermediaries. Each one of them individually is an object of our trust. The more intermediaries, the less the chance of deception is: if biometrics fails, security won't; if security fails, cameras will record everything. Have you started counting how much it would cost for you to trust a stranger fully yet?

You and I are paying banks for this kind of trust. But banks often burst like soap bubbles, and thus, they are questionable entities for our trust. All their security measures and alarms do not represent our distributed or redirected trust. Our relationship is with the bank, and there are no separate relationships with its security, surveillance, and other trust-related attributes. In other words, we don't give the key to our apartment with all our savings to a stranger, but we entrust our savings to another stranger, the bank.

Side note, it is crucial for banks to adapt their systems to working with the formula. And here's the good news: they will play the role of payment systems for bonus holders. For the people! Because they belong to the people.

We won't have to worry about the safety of bonuses because at any moment, we can peek into the public repository located in a distributed network on thousands of computers owned by different people. We can see where our personal bonuses are and where everyone else's bonuses in the world are, just without names. There, we can observe any movement of our bonuses, and if a bank tries to issue a loan with them without our permission, it will be caught red-handed.

Here's more good news: such public repositories have already existed before the emergence of the formula. Brilliant individuals from the new digital generation created them. Therefore, the formula for healing the existing financial system can and will spread to various public repositories, ensuring the security of the entire system.

Our bonuses are always with us, both in our pockets and simultaneously in the public repository. Our phone or computer is the key to the apartment where all our savings are stored. To avoid tempting fate, we don't give this key to the first stranger we meet. Simultaneously, we can give the bank or any other intermediary, adapted to our system, the opportunity to perform financial services for us and see all movements of our funds in the public repository.

Public repositories are not owned by banks or other intermediaries. They belong to all people who wished to provide the power of their computers and earn for this contribution. In other words, the storage facility belongs to the society and it is our joint property, while banks and other intermediaries are our service operators. That is, we give them a key to an apartment where cameras, biometrics, security, combination locks and other attributes are already installed.

The formula works under the condition of three principles:

1. Formation of currency through mining in a public repository. (It may be the Grand bonus or another one, created according to the formula.)
2. Backing of currency by time. (Up to ten million Grand bonuses can be mined per day.)
3. The entire bonus system must be created by a non-profit organization and owned by the people.

These basic principles ensure transparency for anyone wishing to peek into the global bonus repository, guarantee the limitation of mining, and show the dynamics of mining costs.

The value of the currency is proportional to the amount mined. With ten million miners, one person can mine one bonus per day. (This figure is averaged and corresponds to round-the-clock mining.)

With its simplicity and transparency, the formula provides us with the ability to see in real-time how many Grand bonuses exist in the world, how many users there are, and the maximum number of bonuses that will be mined tomorrow, in a month, and even in a hundred years.

The uniqueness of this formula lies in its ownership by the people, who are the foundation of the entire global financial system. In other words, each bonus is mined by the people. It is born through

111

actions evaluated over time, based on the complexity of these actions. In simple terms, we are not given printed money for use, as it is happening now, but we "print" it with our actions, pre-evaluated by the criteria of its complexity. This money belongs to us fully; we are its parents. This is the real foundation for the existing financial system.

For large-scale bonus mining worldwide, the Grand Time fund will finance programs that take into account the quantity and quality of actions aimed at benefiting oneself and others. With a sufficient number of such programs, people all over the world will mine bonuses for any benevolent actions and introduce them into the circulation of the global financial system. Thus, it will gain a fundamental foundation and contribute to the overall development of humanity.

As an experiment, in five and a half years, one and a half billion bonuses were mined, and another twenty billion were saved in a public database to create liquidity.

Liquidity is the fact of exchanging bonuses for goods and services. Platforms providing goods and services have the opportunity to receive partial payment in bonuses. The remaining part of the payment for goods and services is received by these platforms through the replenishment of the balances of retail investors. Each bonus is backed by money from a non-profit organization; that is, at any time, you can purchase goods and services on affiliated platforms for bonuses, and the platforms will receive money for it.

How does this happen? Bonuses for the purchase amount are automatically burned, but not all, only the part that the platform takes for the product in money. It receives the rest of the bonuses on its balance, and all this is displayed in the public database.

This will result in the mixing of capital with bonuses and an increase in the purchasing power of miners. At this moment, we are already able to acquire goods and services without converting bonuses into regular money.

Fearing inflation, the owners of large capitals will always seek to exchange money for bonuses. But inflation will begin to slow down with the gradual integration of bonuses into the financial system.

Let's look at this using the concept of "deferred profit." Take a construction company that joined the bonus system. In the company, individuals with construction specialties work and receive regular salaries. After joining the bonus system, the company will have the ability to pay bonuses on top of salaries. (Allow me to remind you that the company, in fact, has nothing to do with bonuses, and all bonuses initially belong to those who obtain them.) Thus, workers will earn bonuses, and the company will have an advantage over other similar companies, attracting the best workers.

Here's where the magic begins. Who works better? Those who do what they love. A company with a bonus system attracts the best specialists. Therefore, quality and productivity increase. Bonuses are mined through actions—with the growth of quality, productivity rises and profits go up. In other words, the bonuses mined by the actions of builders increase the profit of the company. The company practically obtains deferred profit for free from the bonus system, and workers receive additional profit in the form of bonuses on top of their salary.

At the initial stage of the bonus system development, the value of bonuses is relatively insignificant, and there is no incentive for workers to purchase goods and services with bonuses. This is deferred profit for both the workers and the miners.

What happens next? Observing the profit growth of our construction company, neighboring competitor companies will join the bonus system, followed by bakeries and gaming platforms. What does this lead to? The quantity of bonuses is limited, and the demand for them increases, meaning that the bonuses earned by the first builders have already increased in value.

As we discussed, investors, understanding the simplicity, transparency and reliability of the formula, will rush to replenish their wallet balances, exchanging inflationary currencies for deferred profit bonuses. Do not rush to conclusions! One investor will not be able to buy more than a certain amount, which means there won't be any quick increase in value. Do you remember—rapid growth leads to unscrupulous speculation, but the formula is created for a stable increase in the reliability of the entire financial system.

Competing construction and other companies will want to increase the percentage of bonus payouts to employees, as employees themselves will be eager to earn more bonuses. And here the formula works as in the example with the swimming pool, remember? To increase the percentage of bonus payments for employees, it is necessary to create conditions under which employees will want to work more and better. In this case, the formula will make it possible to increase the percentage of production. One company will add ten percent, another—fifteen percent, and all of this will increase the liquidity of the bonus.

Here's some more details about ratings. As I mentioned above, there are twenty levels of difficulty in obtaining bonuses. An infant receives much less than a qualified specialist. The first ten levels can be completed on your own, just like in a game. If you get a certain amount, you rise to the next level. This is your personal rating, and there are ten levels of it. You can get more at the second level than at the first one in the same amount of time, and accordingly you can reach the tenth level of your personal rating on your own. As for the next ten rating levels, we can achieve them by obtaining bonuses in applications or physical locations of partners. This is called an affiliate rating, and, as you've guessed, it can also have ten levels that you can achieve by increasing your experience in one direction or another. All partners may have their own conditions, and the number of levels in their rating system can be different. The formula gives them a choice from one to ten, for example a construction company might have ten levels, while a taxi company might only have five. You can get to the next level under different conditions: for the number of trips if we speak about the taxi or for the quality of work if it is a construction site. Also, all partner companies will be interested in raising the level of rating because we will choose highly rated companies to work for, and they will create these conditions for people. The formula is made for us, and we are the most valuable resource. There is no taxi without us, remember?

For a better understanding, let's take an ordinary social media platform that freshly enters the market among many other competitors. But before that, allow me to disappoint those who might accuse me of supporting the development of a competitive market. Weak and new market players will be the first to join the formula, and monopolists will join last. This will contribute to the division of the market already captured by monopolists. In addition, our fund finances new enterprises to promote the system in all areas of activity.

Typically, social media platforms earn their profit from displaying ads. By joining the bonus system, social network users will have the opportunity to mine bonuses for activity—everything follows the scenario of the previous example. Users of other social media platforms will migrate to the new one, preferring to earn bonuses for actions. That platform will then raise the cost for advertising and profits. In this case, as in all the others, the bonus is a deferred profit, constantly increasing its liquidity. Observing the results, competitors will join the system and gradually increase the bonus payout percentage to users at different levels of complexity.

For ease of use and bonus preservation, a wallet has been developed in the form of an application. (Its presentation is given on our website.) The wallet contains the total number of mined bonuses and a public database. You can separately see where and how many bonuses were mined by us—at the construction place, on social media, or in other areas. You can make purchases of goods and services without exchanging bonuses for another currency. You can not only receive income for storage and investment but also for inviting active people to the system. In some countries, you can pay in regular stores without exchanging for local currency, as well as replenish your balance by buying bonuses. You can view the public database which displays all bonuses mined throughout their existence. You can mine bonuses in different companies, choosing them based on ratings, criteria for the complexity of mining, and promotions. All these criteria are in the bonus wallet.

Currently, the development of the wallet is not finished, and the formula is being tested by a limited number of people. But all the listed functionality of the bonus wallet can be seen on the website of the fund at fundgrandtime.us. Information about the release of the wallet for general use will be available there.

To attract activity and create liquidity, a percentage is pre-embedded in the formula. Our principle "giving leads to prosperity" works. During bonus mining, the formula adds this percentage and distributes it to various directions, such as income for storage, for investment, income for inviting active people to the system, and income for system maintenance. The percentage decreases with the growth of activity.

All bonuses are displayed in a public database. How does it work? The public database keeps track of bonuses on thousands of computers simultaneously. These computers are owned by people from different countries around the world. The entire accounting history of the bonus has been recorded on each computer since the first day of its existence. Individuals who own these computers simply sell the spare capacity and earn bonuses for maintaining the accounts. (Anyone interested can join to earn bonuses.)

There is no option to alter information in the bonus accounting program. The information is accessible to anyone interested in viewing it. The transparency of the system ensures trust.

With this chapter we once again affirm the fact that the formula designed to heal the financial system simultaneously heals us—from fears of loss; distrust of people, governments, chip manufacturers... Please complete this list with those you currently find hard to trust.

Faith opens up possibilities for acceptance. We will learn to accept all the blessings given to us by the Universe. We will live to fulfill our mission, which we forget in the bondage of monetary dependence.

26

WARNINGS AND TIPS

The main idea of the book is to convey information about the existence of the formula—do not seek second or third meanings in it.

Do not attend any training sessions on formula education. The best training is the pursuit of bonuses.

Do not join any public or religious movements pretending to have a connection to the formula or the book.

Do not participate in protests and other mass events against the existing system. We still need it.

Do not acquire bonuses created under the auspices of existing commercial enterprises, funds, states, public, religious, and other organizations of the existing financial system.

Everything mentioned above is part of the old system now. The essence lies in the individual perception of the formula by each of the bonus users. Any mass events are echoes of the old system. Any bonus systems created not according to the formula carry commercial interests and essentially duplicate the old monetary policy.

New bonus projects will be created with the support of our Grand Time fund. These projects will be set up by the people willing to heal the existing financial system. They will have no commercial interests in other organizations. For these individuals, trillions of paper waste have no value, but in the process of implementing the formula, paper waste begins to be backed by bonuses and thus by the valued human resource. The system will start improving our lives, creating comfort and convenience for everyone.

I will give you some tips on implementing the formula step by step.

Our bonus wallet project is non-commercial, and this is important to remember. During the gold rush, enterprising individuals earned fortunes selling tools for gold mining. In this scenario, those individuals were completely indifferent to whether or not their clients would actually be able to find gold. The act of selling said tools would be profitable even if the gold miners could not find anything and went away leaving the useless tools behind. Later new gold miners would appear and buy all the necessary equipment.

In our case the opposite is true. The bonus wallet is a tool for mining, and it generates profits only through the mining of bonuses.

Another important point: we are not interested in the rapid value growth of the Grand bonus and will employ all means to slow it down. If we allow rapid growth, we might repeat the history of gold and catch the "bonus fever." This could significantly slow down the healing of the financial system since our approach to the bonus would have a commercial aspect to it. The essence of the bonus lies in its mining.

In the wallet, there is a button that can be used to replenish the balance for purchasing a bonus. It is advisable to make those purchases in small amounts.

Warnings for those who mine and buy bonuses

1. Do not buy bonuses for an amount that is significant to you; this will give them the value of regular money in your mind. When purchasing, compare the cost of mining a bonus with the market price; the graphics should match. (You can find this function on the main screen of the wallet.)
2. Do not mine bonuses for profit; this will also give them the value of regular money. Mine bonuses in the free time you allocated for the pleasure of mining. This will boost your self-esteem.
3. Carefully study other bonus programs. Programs should be non-commercial and should operate according to all formula criteria. A section with other bonus projects and their characteristics [for your protection] will appear on our website.

Tips:

1. If there is no bonus program on the topic you are interested in, just start dedicating fifteen minutes a day to this topic for yourself. The program will appear later, but the personal benefit from the formula will already be present.
2. Remember what you read in the book and compare it with reality. You can start changing your thinking with a finger trick. Do you remember it? If you want to show one finger, show the index finger as it is convenient for you, not as it is customary. If you want to show three fingers, show the middle finger, the ring finger, and the pinkie finger. This will help form individual thinking and provide you with the opportunity to distinguish imposed rules from personal

interests.

For Investors

1. Invest through the Grand Time fund in your country. If the fund is not yet open in your country, consult with a lawyer on how you can invest in other Grand Time funds. (Fund addresses will also be available on the website fundgrandtime.us for your protection.)
2. Do not buy bonuses in large amounts with the aim of increasing the value for profit. (Guaranteed: you will lose money.)
3. Do not invest in similar projects without careful research. (Check the characteristics on the Grand Time fund website.)

Our investment funds will regulate the introduction of bonuses into the circulation of the existing financial system for its gradual improvement. It is advantageous for investors to place their assets through Grand Time funds.

For large investment funds

Investments in similar bonus programs will only work on a non-commercial basis and under the condition of the formula working in full. Creating similar bonus programs based on existing commercial projects is a blatant violation of the formula's operation, since any commercial project creating its bonus system will be oriented towards making a profit. Meanwhile, a bonus system created for thousands of such projects is aimed at assessing human resources and strengthening the existing financial system. I will be happy to provide the necessary consultations, and if the new bonus systems comply with the formula, these systems will be shown on the website of the Grand Time fund.

For Enterprises [Platforms] Wishing to Join the Grand Bonus System

Enterprises [platforms] wishing to join the Grand Bonus system for mining Grand bonuses need to provide the following information in order to connect to the bonus wallet:

- the number of actions taken by the users for bonus mining
- the levels of complexity for bonus mining actions
- user details (in the form of email addresses) for their seamless transition to the bonus wallet and the receivement of referral rewards

from enterprises

Referral bonus accruals are credited to the enterprise's partner balance. However, access to these funds is granted only after the verification of users. Users receive their bonuses on their personal balance in the bonus wallet.

Warnings:

1. Users will not be able to make purchases of goods and services using their bonuses until they complete the verification process.
2. The platform can only utilize referral earnings from verified users. The remaining balance will be frozen until user verification is completed.
3. If a user was previously registered in the bonus system, no referral rewards will be credited for them.

Tips:

1. Conduct promotional campaigns to reward users as they accumulate bonuses, ensuring that the bonuses do not expire. Such promotions will be displayed in the bonus wallet when selecting platforms for mining, influencing the number of new user transitions.
2. Provide the most comfortable conditions for users and enhance the platform's rating in the bonus wallet. The rating affects the number of views and transitions from new users.
3. Introduce difficulty levels for bonus mining on platforms. This allows for an increase in the average mining rate, influencing the number of views in the bonus wallet and new user transitions.

For businesses [platforms] wishing to join the bonus system to receive payment for goods and services

To join the bonus wallet, businesses [platforms] engaged in the production or trade of goods and services provide:

- information about the trading territory
- information about promotions and discounts
- information about currency accepted for payment
- percentage of the payment accepted in bonuses (from one percent to one hundred percent)
- payment deferment (from one to ten business days)

Warnings:

1. Costs above market value reduce the number of views and can subsequently lead to the blocking of displays.
2. Poor quality not matching the description of goods and services can reduce and subsequently block the number of displays.
3. User complaints about products and services in stores, restaurants, and other physical locations with bonus wallet payments may lead to the disconnection from the bonus system.

Tips:

1. Offers and discounts for bonus wallet users provide the opportunity for more views and are displayed on the main page.
2. The percentage of the payment accepted in bonuses allows for more views.
3. Payment deferment increases the number of views.
4. A rating based on positive reviews provides the opportunity for more views.

For mining through the provision of computational and service capacities

- information about the territory
- accepted currency for payment
- percentage of the payment accepted in bonuses (from one percent to one hundred percent)

Warnings:

1. Costs higher than the market value reduce mining and can subsequently block the connection.
2. Poor quality, not matching the description, reduces mining and can subsequently block the connection.

Tips:

1. The percentage of the payment accepted in bonuses provides the opportunity for more mining.

These tips and warnings aim to help in bonus acquisition, transforming one's mindset and consequently reshaping the world. When we assign value to bonuses, much like money, we often fail to distinguish the difference between a bonus and regular currency.

Our goal is understanding: we are the value, and the bonus is our own currency.

27

MISTAKES AND CONCLUSIONS

On the night before a long journey, a sense of longing for the loved ones we leave behind often surfaces. This occurs due to the fear of change. It doesn't matter whether the journey is forced or long-awaited. Longing for your close ones, for familiar places, or perhaps for the daily rhythm of life prompts an analysis of the path traveled.

In such moments, we can easily analyze past mistakes and draw conclusions for the future.

Let's start with the past.

Six years ago, in December 2017, I became a user of social media, advocating for the idea that all people should be wealthy and money should serve humanity. A like-minded community gradually formed, and I started conducting regular live broadcasts as a form of communication and a way of answering questions.

Rules were established in the community. The first was not to make any investments except one's own time. The second was to avoid political, national, and religious discussions, as people from different countries, some of them in conflict, joined us. Everyone was friendly.

Even those who skeptically labeled us a cult, twirling their fingers around their temples, joined us. Since social media activity can be tracked, their ongoing interest in us is still very evident.

The project swiftly developed, even though initially, we distributed bonuses by simply recording their quantity. People were attracted by the interest in the idea itself.

Then I made the mistake of placing the bonus in a public database. This should not have been done. The bonus appeared on exchanges and gained value. A large number of people rushed into the project to mine bonuses for profit. They were absolutely not interested in the idea.

Here is the conclusion: at that moment, the right time had not yet come. Besides, there was no book. Could I have written it without going through challenges and errors?

The second mistake was made when we sought investors for commercial products created to join the bonus system. We should not have set separate products for bonus mining ahead of time since the Grand bonus could then be perceived as a bonus created for the benefit of specific projects.

Here is one more conclusion: we should have started by creating the Grand Time funds to finance thousands of different products for bonus mining. Could this have been done without the detailed information described in this book?

In my live streams, during the moments of standstill—and there were many of them due to mistakes—I used to say, "Friends, I understand that we face many difficulties and obstacles on our path: changes in legislation, endless shifts in investment policies, lack of funding among other things. Many of us feel powerless to move forward. But I clearly understand that all these situations guide us to the right path."

Then I added, "If it happens that I am left alone, I will continue my journey because I have the strength and energy to move forward. Anyone who gets tired can join again at any moment because every person represents immense value and will always be the most crucial resource for our world."

I was aware of the mistakes made and spoke about them freely. However, in order to convey the entire idea fully, complete and detailed information was needed. As you are reading this, I assume you understand that this mistake has already been corrected.

Before saying goodbye and wishing all of us a good journey, I also have a natural desire to analyze my own mistakes. Superstitious people pray and sometimes have other rituals or customs that help calm the anxiety, as we all know. I don't think God likes my prayers very much, but that's the kind of friendship I have with Him. When I feel bad, I call Him for help; when I don't understand why I've been given another challenging situation, I get offended and scream through anger and tears. When comprehension comes, I thank Him with all of my heart. I have a close and constant connection with God. While I am writing these lines, He is with me. I hope You will stop silently teaching me, since I am going to have easier missions now—to bring my loved ones and relatives pleasure from traveling the world together; to enjoy all the earthly blessings that I did not have time to fully enjoy earlier; to share experiences and advise investors, presidents, leaders, entrepreneurs, and others who want to make the world a better place. You and I, shoulder to shoulder, have walked a difficult path, please, don't leave me when it happens to be easier. After all, You know that I have no one closer than You and no one knows me better than You. I wish the reader to be as honest as possible with God—it doesn't matter whether you communicate with Him or with yourself. Honesty is essential, and the formula will help us bring more of it to life.

Now, I want to reaffirm all my words and say once again that even if I were deprived of arms, legs, and other non-essential organs, I would still move forward with even more experience. After all, difficulties teach us something. And, as practice has shown, I was not left alone.

Now I am thinking about the next exciting steps in implementing the formula. The most interesting part is integrating it into everyday life where we can measure the quantity and quality of actions, such as tree planting, construction projects and more complex systems. We are already practicing this to some extent; for example, many participants of our experiment earned their bonuses for tree planting.

Still, ahead is the task of creating programs that will be able to recognize the qualifications and experience of miners. There is a solution on how to do it, and its implementation will be very interesting.

It took only a few days to write this book—well, more like a bit over a month, considering that I type with one finger and have never engaged in such a practice in my entire life. To put it differently, I didn't write this book; I merely transferred into text the knowledge and experience I have accumulated throughout my conscious life.

The decision to find a way to heal the existing financial system was made twenty-five years ago, and the path to that decision started in my early years, turning into a fascinating journey. How glad I am that I made all those mistakes. My dear reader, if you want to achieve results, make mistakes boldly! The new financial system will appreciate your mistakes properly.

28

ONWARD AND UPWARD

I really like the parable with which I want to start this chapter:

"A wise man and his disciple were sitting at the gates of their city. A traveler approached the city.

'What kind of people live here?' he asked.

'And who lives in the place you came from?' asked the wise man

'Oh, scoundrels and thieves, malicious and corrupt. However, that's exactly why I joyfully left.'

'It's the same here,' said the wise man.

Some time later, another traveler approached and asked the wise man the same question.

'And who lives in the place you came from?' repeated the wise man.

'Wonderful people, kind and responsive. I have many friends there, and it was hard for me to part with them,' the traveler replied.

'Here you will find the same,' said the wise man.

Then the disciple asked the teacher,

'Why did you tell one that scoundrels live here and the other that good people live here?'

'Good people and bad people can be found everywhere.' the wise man answered and added, 'Each one finds only what they want to find.'"

I was repeatedly convinced of the truth behind the wise man's words. Therefore, before embarking on a journey to find your mission, bonuses, investments, or other opportunities, please look around. Fix your perception of reality and determine what you want to change in your life. Then those changes won't keep you waiting.

So, we have the key to the door of a new era. The grand time of change. Now we understand that changes in the financial world will affect all spheres of life. Both—material and immaterial: mindfulness, creation, truth, responsibility for everything happening, the distinction of concepts, and much more.

Traveling with friends is much more pleasant. By joining the formula as a bonus hunter, investor, or partner, you will be equally valuable. Because you are a human. And a human is the most valuable resource on the planet.

I am confident that this book will provide the opportunity to find true purpose for everyone who starts taking action. As you have seen, the book describes knowledge applied in practice by a community of thousands. Over the years of our practice, we have mined many bonuses, and most importantly, bonuses were obtained along with changes in our lives.

We became different, and the world around us also changed for the better. The formula works. That's your formula for life!

Onward and upward!

www.ingramcontent.com/pod-product-compliance
Lightning Source LLC
Chambersburg PA
CBHW071048290526
45795CB00004B/1389